#One Another

ED&D BOOKS

#OneAnother

A Study of Social Media and College Students

Micheal Pardue

#OneAnother

© 2014 by Micheal Pardue

www.michealpardue.com

Published by:

ED&D BOOKS

Icard, NC

www.educationaldd.com

Scripture quotations are from The Holy Bible, English Standard Version® (ESV®), copyright © 2001 by Crossway, a publishing ministry of Good News Publishers. Used by permission. All rights reserved.

Scripture quotations taken from the New American Standard Bible®, Copyright © 1960, 1962, 1963, 1968, 1971, 1972, 1973, 1975, 1977, 1995 by The Lockman Foundation. Used by permission." (www.Lockman.org)

Cover design by:

www.godditcovered.com

Printed in the United States of America

MICHEAL PARDUE

To my parents,
who provided for my education long past
what we planned or dreamed

CONTENTS

ACKNOWLEDGMENTS

This undertaking would have been an impossible venture without those around me who sacrificed greatly for me to accomplish all that I have. I want to start by thanking my wife, Rachel. She has been unwavering in her support as I have been away at school or locked in my office for the countless hours necessary to produce this dissertation and book. She is by my side at all times and her love is unwavering.

Also, my parents have given me immeasurable support. I have been a student for some twenty-five years now and my parents have been there each step of the way. Their wisdom and encouragement have helped me through times of discouragement and they have made me who I am. I also want to thank my children, Elijah, Jason, Kyle, Kristen, Addelyen, Lilyanna, and Micheal, Jr. for their love. I also could not have finished my doctoral studies without the generosity of my wife's family who made their homes available for me to stay in while I was at the seminary. This generosity could never be over stated.

I want to acknowledge my indebtedness to James Porowski, Greg Lawson, Ken Coley, Larry Purcell, and Travis Bradshaw. They have invested in my life principles and a philosophy of education that I believe will forever be indispensable throughout my ministry in both the church and higher education. Their commitment to God's Word and their faithfulness to their students is a model that will prove hard to replicate.

Those who comprised our Fall 2010 cohort have become true and dear friends. They have been rocks of constant support and made completion of this project possible. Not only have they encouraged, but have shared ideas and helped me to think critically about what I have done. I do not know that I would have been able to finish without Thomas, Cathy, Marcus, Denise, Justin, Merrie, Mike, and Robert. I look forward to seeing how God will send us out from our studies and into our mission.

I also want to thank the schools who made their students available. They strive every day to enrich the lives of their students and I hope that this study will be an aid in that mission. Also, I want to thank Bryan Auday and Sybil Coleman of Gordon College for providing me with the results from their study. Their statistics proved a great aid in my research.

High Shoal Baptist Church made it possible for me to be away during the two years of my doctoral work. They were committed to me and my family during our time there. First Baptist Church of Icard has given me great support during my writing and I am excited to see where God is taking us.

Finally, I know that I, on my own, am incapable of undertaking such a momentous task as the one contained within these pages. The credit for this study goes to Christ and His longsuffering with someone like me. During these months of study and writing I was often reminded of Jesus' words when he said, "Apart from me you can do nothing" (Jn 15:5).

FOREWORD

Man was created in the image of God. Men and women are image bearers of God. God created mankind to worship and glorify Him. In the Garden of Eden, Adam and Eve experienced a dynamic personal relationship with God. As a result of the fall, sin marred the relationship between God and man. Because of God's redeeming love, the relationship between God and man is restored through God's gift of salvation in Jesus Christ. Through Christ's death and resurrection, man can have a personal relationship with God. The personal relationship with God through Jesus Christ provides the foundation for all biblically based human relationships. The one another passages in Scripture provide the framework for Christ-centered relationships.

Micheal Pardue understands the importance of relationships. As a husband, father, pastor, educator and denominational leader, Micheal functions in a variety of ongoing Christ-centered relationships. His commitment to biblical integrity and disciple-making fostered a desire to examine Christ-centered relationships among college and seminary students. In this ground breaking research, Pardue examines students' perceptions of social media's effect on their biblical interpersonal relationships. Understanding that technology and social media have changed the way people communicate, Pardue's cutting edge research launched a one another project website and surveyed over 3600 students from forty schools. The students ranged in age from 17 to over 60 and included undergraduate, graduate and doctoral students. In addition, both online and residential students were surveyed about their social media use.

It should be pointed out that this research group was important because students encounter technology on a daily basis. Pardue contends that these students are more inundated with new technology than any generation before them. Since relationships or community is valued in Christianity and is part of God's design for man, it was important to investigate how students understood the effect of social media on those relationships.

The findings of Pardue's research have big implications for the church and Christian higher education. Anyone who wants to gain a better understanding of Christ and culture should investigate this social media phenomena to gain insights in how to develop biblical community and fellowship among young people in the church and higher education. The biblical mandate to make disciples is timeless. Pardue's ground breaking research demonstrates how social media impacts disciple-making. The reader must view this book from a missional perspective. It is the author's desire that this book glorify God and advance His kingdom.

J. Gregory Lawson, J.D., Ed.D., Ph.D.
October 2014

PREFACE

This book has been a labor of love and hate. Being a dissertation, it required long hours, away from my family, stuck in a library, combing through journal articles. It was tedious and at times frustrating.

However, it was also an exciting adventure. I learned a lot about Christian community and myself along the way. I was able to explore two highly relevant phenomenon at the same time: the recent advent of social media and Christian community. It has made a meteoric rise to near universal use in our culture. It has revolutionized many things, foremost, how we communicate.

I was able to study this modern marvel in conjunction with the ancient sensation of Christian community. For nearly 2,000 years the disciples of Jesus Christ have shared a unique bond, drawn together by the blood of the Savior and indwelling of the Holy Spirit.

This book reports the results of my 2012 study of the perceived effect social media is having on Christian college and seminary students.

I believe these results are helpful in seeing how these students understand what social media is doing to their relationships. There were some encouraging results. Most of the students had used social media to both pray with someone else and share their faith. We need to do a lot more research in this area. What does that mean and how do we take advantage? Social media will remain an evolving revolution for the foreseeable future. There will be rapid advances and we will struggle to keep up. However, I believe we cannot stand idly by.

Over the last two years, I have chaired a committee of the Baptist State Convention of North Carolina that oversees communication throughout the more than 4,000 churches that comprise the convention. Not a single meeting passed without the convention staff or the members of the committee introducing us to new platforms of communication that are changing how we connect with one another. The question before us will always be "How do we make use of this technology to reach others with the Gospel of Christ?" My hope is that this study will serve that purpose and do so to the glory of our Heavenly Father.

Dr. Micheal S. Pardue
Icard, NC
November 2014

#ONEANOTHER

1 THE PROBLEM AND ITS SETTING

Introduction

Before the creation of the world, a deep, personal relationship was present within the three Persons of the Trinity. Jesus, who was with God in creation (Jn 1:1-3), prays that all believers would be one so that the world may believe (Jn 17:21). This "togetherness" of the Trinity is evident in Genesis 1:26 with: **[L]et us make man in our own image.** Father, Son, and Holy Spirit work as one to create all that has been made (Hammett, 2007). This, coupled with God's proclamation from Genesis 2:18, **It is not good that the man should be alone; I will make him a helper fit for him**, shows that God is a relational being and created humans with the same desire.

There are several distinct marks of biblical interpersonal relationships (BIR) in the Scriptures. These marks may look somewhat different among various believers, but they are all commands that must be present in a church that is healthy and seeking to follow Christ's will. These are not attributes that individual Christians can cultivate on their own. John Hammett writes, "The theological motif that underlies the doctrine of community is that it must be a divine creation, not a human achievement" (Hammett, 2007, p. 398). He sees this motif developing in three ways throughout the whole of Scripture:

- God has made the promise **"I will be their God, and they will be my people."**
- The Holy Spirit is sent to dwell in the hearts of people. Fellowship is not found in the New Testament until the arrival of the Spirit at Pentecost.
- Christ's death is "the bringer of reconciliation and the ultimate source of the church's unity and community" (Hammett, 2007, pp. 398-99)

The Bible indicates that believers should desire that God would develop within their community of faith these principles so that they can enjoy the privilege of fellowship within the community of Christ. The fellowship that is displayed in the BIR of the early Church has several distinct characteristics. BIR involves love that is brotherly, free of judgment, humble, not envious, forgiving, patient, honest, and kind.

Relationships, of course, are not limited to believers. Human beings require interaction with other people. In fact, a person who avoids relationships may be diagnosed with Schizoid Personality Disorder. The *Diagnostic and Statistical Manual of Mental Disorders* (2000) says that a person with this disorder will have "a pervasive pattern of detachment from social relationships and a restricted range of expression of emotions in interpersonal settings, beginning in early adulthood and present in a variety of contexts."

Seeking relationships with others, on the other hand, is encouraged by psychology. Brehem, Miller, Perlman, and Campbell (2002) write:

Intimate relationships fulfill basic human needs for belonging and caring, they involve strong emotional attachments to others, and often interdependence with others as well. It is now well known that the single best protection anyone can have against the risks of many mental and physical illnesses is being part of a viable social support network. Intimate relationships provide meaningful, often enduring, networks of social support, of other people we can call upon when distressed, and in turn give aid and care to others when they are in need. (p. xv)

Berkman and Glass (2000) continue this idea, writing, "Across the life span, people who have few friends or lovers have much higher mortality rates than do those who are closely connected to caring partners" (p. 6).

The Bible envisions deep, meaningful relationships among Christians. It is apparent, even simply skimming the Scriptures, that those who are called of God enter into a relationship with Him and fellow believers. This relationship stands in contrast to the relationships among people who are outside of God's family. There is a sense of sacrifice and a strong theme of mutual love that permeates the Scripture when examples are given of men and women who are in communion with both God and His followers. These BIR have definite characteristics that must be present for these relationships to be healthy. This study examined not *if* there exists a need for these relationships, that fact was assumed. It examined whether or not believers in Christ regard the recent phenomenon of social media as having an effect on those relationships that are foundational to the Christian life and experience. This researcher asked Christian college and seminary students across North American to consider that very question.

Research Purpose

Technology and social media have changed the way people communicate. According to a Pew Study (2011), in the major countries of the world, most people are using technology on a daily basis, with 85% using cell phones and 75% of those same people sending text messages. At least one in four people in 15 of the world's largest countries use social media regularly. In the U.S., 73% of 18-29 year-olds use their cell phone to access the Internet. Sixty-six percent of all Americans are using social media (Barna, 2008). Human beings seem to be more connected than ever.

However, is this "connection" real? Sherry Turkle (2011), noted MIT psychologist who has studied new technologies for more than thirty years, laments that the use of technology may be having a different outcome than its perceived effect:

> We are offered robots and a whole world of machine-mediated relationships on networked devices. As we instant message, email, text, and twitter, technology redraws the boundaries between intimacy and solitude. We talk of getting "rid" of our emails, as though these notes are so much excess baggage. Teenagers avoid making telephone calls, fearful that they will "reveal too much." They would rather text than talk. Adults, too, choose keyboards over the human voice. It is more efficient, they say. Things that happen in "real time" take too much time. Tethered to technology, we are shaken when that world "unplugged" does not signify, does not satisfy. After an evening of avatar-to-avatar life and, in the next, curiously isolated, in tenuous complicity with strangers. We build a following on Facebook or MySpace and wonder to what degree our followers are friends. We recreated ourselves as online personae and give ourselves new bodies, homes, jobs, and romances. Yet, suddenly, in the half-light of virtual community, we may feel utterly alone. As we distribute

ourselves, we may abandon ourselves. Sometimes people experience no sense of having communicated after hours of connection. And they report feelings of closeness when they are paying little attention. In all of this, there is a nagging question: Does virtual intimacy degrade our experience of the other kind and indeed, of all encounters, of any kind? (pp. 11-12)

Turkle sees a trend of people connected but alone. She writes of a grandmother-granddaughter relationship that because of the great distances between them is most often experienced over Skype. Because the granddaughter is often working on other tasks while also speaking with her grandmother, Turkle observes that they "were more connected than they had ever been before, but at the same time, each was alone" (p. 14).

Christians are not immune from experiencing this new "connectedness." The Church already has an online presence. According to statistics from 2008, more than 6 in 10 Protestant churches have an online presence and more than half contact some large segment of their membership with email (Barna, 2008). Has this foray into the cyber world strengthened Christian relationships? Do Christians believe that they are closer and more connected to their fellow believers? What effect does that connectivity through social media have on interpersonal relationships? The answers to those questions are vital for believers to consider as more and more is done to connect people through the use of social media.

Tim Challis (2011), noted pastor and blogger, asks his readers, presumably from the Church, if they understand what is going on. "We now consider community what was previously mere *communication*....Our perception of community is becoming disembodied, a product of mediated communication based on shared interest rather than a product of face-to-face communication based on shared space" (p. 103). Challis has concerns about what current technology is doing to the Church and Christians. It challenges, for instance, authority as defined in Scripture, taking it away from God and those who have been entrusted with His message, and gives it to anyone who can set up a blog or website. These realities demand that the Church explore what is happening when Christians step into the virtual world of social media. Even more so, with the advent of churches that fully function online, it is necessary to know how participants in the Christian faith understand the media that has enveloped them.

Therefore, because of the data available about who is consuming the most social media, the purpose for this researcher was to discover if North American Christian college and seminary students (NACCSS) perceive a positive or negative impact on their relationships through the use of social media. This study has shed light on whether or not this subset of the Christian population is being affected by the ever-increasing use of social media. This research sought to help churches and Bible colleges assess where and how they can use social media to build strong BIRs in their particular settings.

Research Questions and Sub-Problems

The following questions served as the basis for the development for the survey instrumental, the collection of data and the subsequent analysis of the collected data:

- What, if any, is the positive relationship between social media use and biblical interpersonal relationships as perceived by North American Christian college and seminary students?
- What, if any, is the negative relationship between social media use and biblical interpersonal relationships as perceived by North American Christian college and seminary students?

- What is the perceived effect of social media use on biblical interpersonal relationships among North American Christian college and seminary students?

From the research questions, there arose eight sub-problems that made it possible to answer the research questions. They are:

- What, if any, is the relationship between time spent in church activities and the perception of the effect of social media use on biblical interpersonal relationships among North American Christian college and seminary students?
- What, if any, is the relationship between time spent using social media and the perception of the effect of social media use on biblical interpersonal relationships among North American Christian college and seminary students?
- What, if any, is the relationship between gender and the perception of the effect of social media use on biblical interpersonal relationships among North American Christian college and seminary students?
- What, if any, is the relationship between age and the perception of the effect of social media use on biblical interpersonal relationships among North American Christian college and seminary students?
- What, if any, is the relationship between the whether or not a subject has shared his/her faith through social media and the perception of the effect of social media use on biblical interpersonal relationships among North American Christian college and seminary students?
- What, if any, is the relationship between the whether or not a subject has prayed with someone through social media and the perception of the effect of social media use on biblical interpersonal relationships among North American Christian

college and seminary students?

Research Hypotheses

Before beginning the study, the researcher drew the following hypotheses that correlate to the research questions.

- What, if any, is the positive relationship between social media use and biblical interpersonal relationships as perceived by North American Christian college and seminary students? H: There will be multiple characteristics of biblical interpersonal relationships that students will see as having a positive relationship with the use of social media.
- What, if any is the negative relationship between social media use and biblical interpersonal relationships as perceived by North American Christian college and seminary students? H: There will be multiple characteristics of biblical interpersonal relationships that students will see as having a negative relationship with the use of social media.
- What is the perceived effect of social media use on biblical interpersonal relationships among North American Christian college and seminary students? H: The overall perception of social media's effect on biblical interpersonal relationships will be positive.

This researcher also drew the following hypotheses concerning the sub-problems associated with the research questions.

- What, if any, is the relationship between time spent in church activities and the perception of the effect of social media use on biblical interpersonal relationships among North American Christian college and seminary students? H: Students who spend more time at church will have a more negative overall perception of the effect of social media on their biblical interpersonal relationships. Therefore, time spent in church activities will be a significant factor in the determining a student's perception of the effect of social media use on biblical interpersonal relationships. There will be a negative correlation between the increase of time spent in church activities and a more negative view of the effect of social media on biblical interpersonal relationships.

▪ What, if any, is the relationship between time spent using social media and the perception of the effect of social media use on biblical interpersonal relationships among North American Christian college and seminary students?

H: Students who spend more time using social media will have a more positive overall perception of the effect of social media use on biblical interpersonal relationships. Therefore, time spent using social media will be a significant factor in the determining a student's perception of the effect of social media use on biblical interpersonal relationships. There will be a positive correlation between the increase of time spent using social media and a more positive view of the effect of social media on biblical interpersonal relationships.

▪ What, if any, is the relationship between gender and the perception of the effect of social media use on biblical interpersonal relationships among North American Christian college and seminary students?

H: Gender will not affect student's perception of social media's effect on biblical interpersonal relationships. Therefore, time spent using social media will be a significant factor in the determining a student's perception of the effect of social media use on biblical interpersonal relationships.

▪ What, if any, is the relationship between age and the perception of the effect of social media use on biblical interpersonal relationships among North American Christian college and seminary students?

H: Students who are younger will have a more positive overall perception of the effect of social media use on biblical interpersonal relationships. Therefore, age will be a significant factor in the determining a student's perception of the effect of social media use on biblical interpersonal relationships. There will be a negative correlation between the increase of age and a more positive view of the effect of social media on biblical interpersonal relationships.

▪ What, if any, is the relationship between the whether or not a subject has shared his/her faith through social media and the perception of the effect of social media use on biblical interpersonal relationships among North American Christian college and seminary students?

H: Students who have shared their faith through social media will have a more positive overall perception of the effect of social media use on biblical interpersonal relationships. Therefore, having shared one's faith through social media will be a significant factor in the determining a student's perception of the effect of social media use on biblical interpersonal relationships. There will be a positive correlation between sharing one's faith and a more positive view of the effect of social media on biblical interpersonal relationships.

▪ What, if any, is the relationship between the whether or not a subject has prayed with someone through social media and the perception of the effect of social media use on biblical interpersonal relationships among North American Christian college and seminary students?

H: Students who have prayed with someone through social media will have a more positive overall perception of the effect of social media use on biblical interpersonal relationships. Therefore, having prayed with someone through social media will be a significant factor in the determining a student's perception of the effect of social media use on biblical interpersonal relationships. There will be a positive correlation between having prayed with someone and a more positive view of the effect of social media on biblical interpersonal relationships.

Delimitations of the Study

There were several delimitations of this study, involving both the biblical theology behind the definition of BIR and the type of students who would be used to garner the data that was examined. Theologically, the definition of BIR was limited to teachings found in the New Testament. More specifically, it focused on the concepts brought out in the "one another" sayings of the Epistles. Of course, this does not make them independent of the Old Testament or the Gospels since as all the New Testament Epistles build off of prior Scriptures.

In the process of selecting schools to participate, only schools that self-identified as Christian were contacted about possible participation in the study. In regards to the subjects used for the study, only responses from self-described Christians were used. Since this study did not examine the relationships between Christians and non-Christians, any subject who indicated he/she was not Christian did not have their responses factored into the data analysis. In addition, only current students were used. In some instances, alumni of the various participating institutions became aware of the study and filled out the online questionnaire. However, because they did not fall under the scope of the study, their responses were disallowed during the data analysis.

Terminology

Interpersonal relationships: Interpersonal relationships are those physiological, sociological, psychological connections that two or more people share.

Biblical interpersonal relationships: Biblical interpersonal relationships are the ideal relationships between Christians as set forth in the Epistles of the New Testament. While it is true that completely ideal relationships do not exist, the model is presented in Scripture and is to be sought by the Christian.

Social media: Social media is any electronic medium through which people communicate with one another.

Research Assumptions

There are several things that the researcher assumed while planning and executing the research. The first is that the Bible presents God's perfect design for interpersonal relationships among humans in general and Christians specifically. The questions that test subjects were asked are derived from a biblical analysis of interpersonal relationships. This research assumed that technology and social media are being used in the interpersonal relationships of NACCSS. The researcher also assumed that the subjects were honest in indicating they were Christians and honest in their self-evaluation of their church attendance and social media usage. The researcher also assumed they were mature enough to understand the meaning of the biblical characteristics of interpersonal relationships.

Research Methods

The questionnaire used for this study was designed in two parts. The first gathered demographic data which the researcher used to divide the respondents in to groups so that conclusions could be drawn about what variables were affecting the answers given by the respondents. Second, respondents were asked to rank on a Likert scale their perceptions on social media's effect on fifteen areas identified as essential to biblical interpersonal relationships. These characteristics of BIR were identified through 15 of the "one another sayings" from the New Testament.

To gather the needed data for this study, the researcher contacted more than 300 hundred self-described Christian colleges and seminaries across the United States and Canada. These schools were asked to participate in the study by sending out a link to the researcher's questionnaire. Forty schools participated in the study and 3,645 questionnaires were collected.

The survey was posted at http://www.oneanotherproject.org and respondents were able to access this website at their leisure. Each school chose to send out the link in the way in which they believed would best reach their students. The schools were provided with a template email that they could format into whatever medium best suited their needs.

The data was then examined using IBM's SPSS Statistics 20. The means of results from the Likert scale questions were compared with the demographic information gathered from the respondents. These comparisons led to the results reported in Chapter Four.

2 LITERATURE REVIEW

Introduction

This chapter is a review of precedent literature that was used to build the instrument to test the perceived effect of social media on the biblical interpersonal relationships (BIR) of North American Christian college and seminary students (NACCSS). To do this it was necessary to examine literature in two areas:

- The researcher examined theologically relevant material to construct the characteristics of BIR. To do this, both theological works directly related to BIR and commentaries on the relevant passages that prescribed BIR were examined. Often, in contemporary theological works, BIR is thought of in the language of and synonymous with the term *community*.
- The researcher also examined secular and Christian writings on the effect of social media on relationships.

Theological Foundation

It is apparent, even when skimming Scripture, that those who are called of God enter into a relationship both with God and fellow believers that stands in contrast to the relationships among people who are outside of God's family. There is a sense of sacrifice and a strong theme of mutual love that permeates the Scriptures when examples are given of men and women who are in communion with God and His followers. This section, by investigating these themes, seeks to: (1) define BIR, (2) ascertain if BIR is actually prescribed in Scripture or is simply described, and (3), if community is prescribed, answer the question, "what are marks of proper BIR in a contemporary New Testament church?" This will be accomplished by looking at a number of Biblical texts about BIR with the goal of putting together a theology for the attributes of BIR.

The English word *community* is not prevalent in most Bible translations. *Community* does not appear in the ESV, NLT, or the KJV. The NIV uses "community" numerous times in the O.T. [Gn 28:3; 48:4; Ex 12:3, 20, 47; 16:1-10; Lv 16:5; Nm 1:2; Jos 22:17] referring to the nation of Israel. *Community* appears once in the NASB, but not in relation to communion among God's children. *Fellowship*, however, is found in English translations, both modern and dated. However, the word *fellowship* (κοινωνία) is applicable to the theology of community, and it will be these two words, the English *fellowship* and the Greek κοινωνία that will be examined in ascertaining the meaning of *community*. These two words are defined below.

What are Biblical Interpersonal Relationships and Does the Bible Prescribe these Relationships for All Believers

The questions, what are BIR and does the Bible prescribe them, can and must be answered together. A non-Biblical definition of *community* will serve little purpose for determining if the Bible prescribes BIR for contemporary believers. However, as will be clear from looking at the Bible's teaching on BIR, human beings are relational creatures and therefore there are some similarities within the actions of relationships for both believers and non-believers.

For instance, people tend to enjoy the company of other people. This stems from the words of God in Genesis 2:18 ESV, **It is not good that the man should be alone; I will make him a helper fit for him.** Human beings, unless they have some type of mental or physical illness, enjoy and desire relationships with others. This is commonly understood in secular psychology. A person who avoids relationships may be diagnosed with Schizoid personality disorder. The *Diagnostic and Statistical Manual of Mental Disorders* (2000) says that a person with this disorder will have "a pervasive pattern of detachment from social relationships and a restricted range of expression of emotions in interpersonal settings, beginning in early adulthood and present in a variety of contexts." Seeking relationships with others, on the other hand, is encouraged by psychology. Brehem, Miller, Perlman, and Campbell (2002) write:

> Intimate relationships fulfill basic human needs for belonging and caring, they involve strong emotional attachments to others, and often interdependence with others as well. It is now well known that the single best protection anyone can have against the risks of many mental and physical illnesses is being part of a viable social support network. Intimate relationships provide meaningful, often enduring, networks of social support, of other people we can call upon when distressed, and in turn give aid and care to others when they are in need"(p. xv). "Across the life span, people who have few friends or lovers have much higher mortality rates than do those who are closely connected to caring partners. (Berkman & Glass, 2000)

In Christian relationships this desire should be intense because of the prospect of genuine relationships that can be found only through the salvation of Christ and the leadership of the Holy Spirit. Bonhoeffer (1954) wrote:

> The believer feels no shame, as though he were still living too much in the flesh, when he yearns for the physical presence of other Christians. Man was created a body, the Son of God appeared on earth in the body, he was raised in the body, in the sacrament the believer receives the Lord Christ in the body, and the resurrection of the dead will bring about the perfected fellowship of God's spiritual-physical creatures. The believer therefore lauds the Creator, the Redeemer, God, Father, Son and Holy Spirit, for the bodily presence of a brother. (pp. 19-20)

Christians should have a strong desire to be around likeminded believers. "It may be argued that one aspect of being made in God's image is being made for community" (Hammett, 2007, p. 368).

This is not to say, however, that secular community is comparable to the BIR that the Scriptures describe (Schaeffer, 1998). Genuine BIR is "a community formed by the Spirit under the sovereign lordship of the exalted Christ" (Moore, 2004, p. 155).

Biblical interpersonal relationships defined. To define BIR, it is important to examine the word *fellowship* (κοινωνία). Bock (2007) writes of this word: "Luke points to fellowship to underscore the personal interactive character of relationships in the early church at all levels....There is a real sense of connection to, between, and for each other" McRay (2001) points out that the "basic meaning conveyed by the Greek term *koinōnia* is that of participation. Both fellowship and communion, as translations of this term, are to be understood in this light."

Grenz (1996) has defined community as "a reconciled people who enjoy fellowship with him (meaning God), with one another, and ultimately with all creation" (p. 23). This definition reveals the two primary means of fellowship for human beings—vertical and horizontal. Relationships throughout the Bible are developed first with God and then with other people. As argued above, secular relationships pale in comparison to the relationships that are available to those in communion with God. The relationship with God makes it possible for believers with different backgrounds and beliefs to fellowship together in Christ. The *Evangelical Dictionary of Theology* expands on this idea as follows:

> The unity in the fellowship of the early church was not based upon uniformity of thought and practice, except where limits of immorality or rejection of the confession of Christ were involved. The capacity to fellowship with one with whom there were disagreements extended beyond the cooperate church into the home itself. (McRay, 2001)

Therefore, it can be seen that BIR involves a bond between believers that overcomes disagreements and involves relationships that extend outside the church.

BIR, though a contemporary phraseology, is not a new concept. The *Philadelphia Baptist Confession of Faith*, which was adopted by the Philadelphia Baptist Association in 1742, says this about BIR:

> All saints that are united to Jesus Christ as their Head, by His Spirit, and faith, although they are not made thereby one person with Him, have fellowship in His graces, sufferings, death, resurrection and glory; and being united to one another in love, they have communion in each others [sic] gifts and graces, and are obliged to the performance of such duties, public and private, in an orderly way, as do conduce to their

mutual good, both inward and outward man....Saints by profession, are bound to maintain a holy fellowship and communion in the worship of God, and in performing such other spiritual services, as tend to their mutual edification; as also in relieving each other in outward things, according to their several abilities; which communion, according to the rule of the gospel, though especially to be exercised by them, in the relations wherein they stand, whether in families, or in churches, yet as God offereth opportunity, is to be extended to all the household of faith, even all those who in every place call upon the Name of Jesus; nevertheless their communion one with another as saints, doth not take away, or infringe the title or property which each man hath in his goods and possessions. (2007, p. 64)

This confession of faith calls for a community of believers who share in each other's joys and burdens. This confession even goes so far as to call fellowship mandated. This will be examined further under *BIR Prescribed*.

Fellowship cannot, as it often is, be understood as mere time together, though that is most certainly involved. Oftentimes churches have "fellowship halls" or "fellowship meals" or "fellowship greeting times." Fellowship and BIR may be present and cultivated in these buildings and scheduled events, but they do not define fellowship. The converse is true. Genuine fellowship and BIR should be the desired outcome of any event that takes place in all church buildings, should be the natural outflow that leads to meals together, and should be obvious to everyone gathered for corporate worship in a time set aside for greetings (Segler & Bradley, 2006, p. 85; Malphurs, 2007, p. 81).

Having examined several sources, this writer discovered that BIR are a broad idea. It is, however, a state of being that God desires to permeate the lives of His children. True BIR can only take place among believers and it will be marked by their love for God which will be demonstrated in love for one another and the world around them. It has been said that imitation is the greatest form of flattery. In BIR, Christians will honor and glorify Christ by imitating His love for BIR as displayed in both His heavenly and earthly relationships.

Biblical interpersonal relationships described. Having been defined, it is important to examine the Biblical record for a description of BIR. Beginning even before the creation of the world, an interpersonal relationship was present within the three Persons of the Trinity. Jesus, who was with God in creation (Jn 1:1-3), prays that all believers would **be one** (in unity) **just as you, Father, are in me, and I in you, that they also may be in us, so that the world may believe that you have sent me** (Jn 17:21). This "togetherness" of the Trinity is evident in Genesis 1:26 with **let us make man in our own image.** Father, Son, and Holy Spirit work as one to create all that has been made (Hammett, 2007). This coupled with God's proclamation mentioned above from Genesis 2:18 shows that God is a relational being and created humans with the same desire.

The sin of humanity broke the intimate community present before the Fall between God and the pinnacle of His creation, Adam and Eve. This broken relationship limits man's access to God. Walton (2001) writes:

> In Israel, while there was undoubtedly a recognition of the inherent nature of sin, the biggest problem of the Fall was not concentrated in the change in human nature or the heart condition but in the loss of access to the presence of God and the reduced ability to participate in the blessing. (p. 231)

This meant that community was no longer possible with God, at least in the same manner it had been. "A thick veil separated the people from God's presence" (Norman, 2005, p. 95) once the temple was built. No longer could just any person have direct access to God. In fact, the presence of God often scared people in the Old Testament (Ex 30:18-19). Though the Law and the sacrifice represented a means of restoration of the relationship that existed before the Fall, it was by no means perfect (Isa 1:11; Rm 3:20).

The possibility for community with God and others changed at the cross. "The work of the cross restores our relationship with God (Eph 2:16) but also creates a new community among humans—the church" (Hammett, 2007, p. 368). This is beautifully pictured when the veil that separated the Jews from the presence of God in the Holy of Holies is torn from top to bottom after Jesus' death (Mt 27:51; Mk 15:38; Lk 23:45). No longer would human sinfulness demand that God separate Himself from humanity because through Christ there is reconciliation available to those who will believe (Eph 2:14-16). These BIR, available through Christ's atoning work on the cross, are seen almost immediately after His ascension.

Acts 2 provides a good representation of what BIR looked like among the earliest Christians. Luke tells his readers that those who were added to the number of disciples continually devote themselves to the apostles' teaching and also to fellowship (Acts 2:41-42). Luke goes on to write that: **they were together and had all things in common** (Acts 2:44). **They were of one mind and broke bread from house to house taking their meals together with gladness and sincerity of heart, praising God and having favor with all people** (Acts 2:46). Luke then finishes this section by showing that this lifestyle of BIR is the sovereign will of God when he states: **And the Lord was adding to their number day by day those who were being saved** (Acts 2:47). BIR are not only beneficial for the Christian, but is ultimately for the work of the Kingdom. From the beginning, writes Ladd (1974), there has been a clear call for fellowship among believers. He states:

One of the most striking elements in the life of the primitive churches was their sense of fellowship. **'They devoted themselves to the apostles' teaching and fellowship'** ([Acts] 2:42). The several statements that the early Christians were 'together' ([Acts] 2:44, 47) designate the quality of their fellowship as much as their common assemblage. The early Christians were conscious of being bound together because they were bound to Christ. They were an eschatological people not only because they were called to inherit the eschatological Kingdom but because they had already experienced the blessings of the messianic era. In a sense, their fellowship was a foretaste of the fellowship of the eschatological Kingdom, displayed in history in the midst of Judaism. It was inconceivable that a believer should be such in isolation. To be a believer meant to share with other believers the life of the coming age, to be a believer in fellowship, to be in the ekklēsia. (p. 350-51)

This demonstrates why the writers of the New Testament would spend so much time talking about the relationship among believers. Christianity is, by nature, a relational faith; first and foremost is the believer's relationship with Christ, but, as an outflow, relationships with others.

The Apostle Paul writes extensively about the BIR of believers in his letters to the various churches. Several of these passages will be discussed below, but it is clear that Paul has a high view of importance of relationships among believers. He frequently chastises those who are contentious (Ti 3:10). He laments when there are divisions among the brethren (1 Cor 11:18-19). Paul desperately wants unity among believers and his teaching on BIR makes that clear (Eph 4:1-3).

1 John 1:1-10 also provides an accessible description of what BIR are and how they are possible. John writes, **[I]f we walk in the**

Light as He Himself is in the Light, we have fellowship with one another (1 Jn 1:7). Therefore, one must be in fellowship with Christ, through His blood, which cleanses the believer of sins (1 Jn 1:7). A believer, having been cleansed of his sins, will then be able to have community with Christ in truth (1 Jn 1:6). He will also have BIR with other believers who are communing with the Father, and with His Son Jesus Christ (1 Jn 1:3). Stott writes:

> The fellowship created by Christ in the days of his flesh within the apostolic band, and deepened by the coming of the Spirit at Pentecost, was not to be limited to them. It was to extend to the next generation (***that you also may have fellowship with us***), and so on down the ages. . . . The purpose of the proclamation of the gospel is, therefore, stated in terms not of salvation but of *fellowship*. Yet, properly understood, this is the meaning of salvation in its widest embrace, including reconciliation to God in Christ. (Stott, 1989, p. 68)

Fellowship, therefore, is uniquely Christian because only those who are children of God are able to partake in it. Fellowship is communion, both with the Trinity and among those who have also been forgiven by His blood.

BIR does not end with the Parousia of Christ. In fact, BIR will be perfected when the Kingdom of God is fully consummated. John records in Revelation 5:9 that he saw the four living creatures and the twenty-four elders bowing before the Lamb and: **they sang a new song, saying, 'Worthy are you to take the scroll and to open its seals, for you were slain, and by your blood you ransomed people for God from every tribe and language and people and nation'** (Rev 5:9). In Heaven, people from every nation of the world will be in communion with both Christ (Isa 60:19; 2 Cor 5:8; Phil

1:23; 1 Thes 4:17) and each other (Eph 2:19, 3:14; Heb 11:13; Rev 7:9). The BIR that God desires for His church is a foretaste of community in eternity (Grenz, 1996, pp. 252-300).

Biblical interpersonal relationships prescribed. The writer of Hebrews gives one of the clearest exhortations that fellowship with other believers in community is mandated in Scripture when he writes:

> **And let us consider how to stir up one another to love and good works, not neglecting to meet together, as is the habit of some, but encouraging one another, and all the more as you see the Day drawing near.** (Heb 10:24-25)

Some in his day were apparently prone to neglecting fellowship with other believers—making it their habit. He exhorts his readers to stir up one another to love and good works. In so doing they will encourage one another and be more prepared for the Day of the Lord. This passage of Scripture has led many churches (especially churches of previous generations) to adopt a discipline policy for those who neglect "to meet together." Driscoll & Breshears (2010) list "when a Christian is not consistently in community" as a reason for discipline from the church body. They cite Hebrews 10:24-25 as reasoning for this discipline (p. 329). The authors also link this text and the command to gather together with the Great Commandment of Christ in the Gospels (p. 311). The practice of discipline for absenteeism was common in the church in the 19th century as well. For example, this writer's own church's history records that a rule once existed that stated, ". . . [I]f a member failed to attend church and failed to contribute to the church programs for a period of one year, he automatically excluded himself" (Hendricks, 1986, p. 48).

Witmer (2010) writes of Hebrews 10:24-25 that, "This represents not merely a commitment to be in worship *somewhere,* but to be in attendance with the other members of . . . [a] particular flock" (p. 200). Flock is a good term for community because a sheep separated from its flock has a similar chance of survival as a Christian outside of her community.

Leeman (2010) sees an intrinsic connection between neglect of BIR and sin in the life of a believer. He writes:

> The person who neglects meeting with the saints is on his way toward God's judgment, and the dim picture of that judgment represented by church discipline is a merciful act of warning. When members stop attending a church and don't join another one, they are often sinning or on their way to sinning. There's something in their life they don't want to be seen. There's accountability and love they would prefer to be without. (p. 316)

Continuing to develop the idea of BIR, the writer of Hebrews goes on to say, **Therefore let us be grateful for receiving a kingdom that cannot be shaken, and thus let us offer to God acceptable worship, with reverence and awe, for our God is a consuming fire** (Heb 12:28-29). He then goes on to say that the way this is done, the way that Christians are grateful for receiving this kingdom, is through the BIR that this kingdom has created. He says, **Let brotherly love continue** (Heb 13:1). This idea of brotherly love will be developed below under the first mark of BIR, but the writer in Hebrews uses this phrase to begin what Akin (2009) has called "Marks of a Healthy Community of Faith." The entire thirteenth chapter of Hebrews discusses, in part, what a healthy Biblical community will look like. Several of these topics will be discussed below under *Characteristics of BIR.*

If these attributes are present, the church is a place the believer desires to be. Malphurs (2007) has rightly said that "believers and unbelievers alike—especially younger ones—yearn for this kind of relationship [deep fellowship] and look for it within the church" (p. 81). This gives the church a prime opportunity to foster these relationships and meet the spiritual and social needs of those in the community of faith. At the same time, Malphurs gives this warning:

> If they don't find it there [meaning the church], they look for it in other places outside the church, such as the workplace, sports, clubs, and bars. Churches that desire to reach people and minister to them, especially younger believers, need ministries that address this deeply felt need for fellowship. (p. 81)

BIR and fellowship are thus Biblically described and prescribed, with some overlap between the prescriptions and descriptions.

Seeing how the Bible both describes and prescribes BIR, believers may ask why there is a void in fellowship among Christians. Hammett (2007) strikes at the heart of this question when he writes:

> By their very nature, churches are called to be a community. But human sinfulness, along with cultural obstacles, such as individualism and the consumer culture, as well as religious obstacles such as churches so large individuals fall between the cracks or ignorance of the Biblical teaching on community, has left many churches sorely lacking in this area. (p. 406)

Sin and culture keep believers from rejoicing with one another, in Christ, about the great work He is doing in their lives. Sin and culture also keep Christians from leaning on one another, in Christ, and sharing the burdens in their lives together. Believers should strive hard to keep sin and culture from ruining the relationships God wants them to have with each other.

Characteristics of biblical interpersonal relationships. These characteristics represent attributes of BIR, not activities. Activities such as cooperate worship, prayer, mission activities, charitable endeavors, Bible study, meals, trips, various social ministries, and other programs will, and arguably must, be present within the community of the Church and local congregations. The marks presented below are attributes that must be present within these activities for BIR to take place. Therefore, prayer, for example, must be done in love, without pride, and both seeking and giving forgiveness. Dever (2004) gives a number of activities that will take place inside a healthy Biblical community. Many of these activities are a direct result of the presence of these attributes mentioned above.

There are several distinct marks of BIR in the Scriptures. These marks will take different shapes among different believers, but they are all commands that must be present in the church that is seeking to follow Christ's will. These are not attributes that individual Christians can cultivate on their own. "The theological motif that underlies the doctrine of community is that it must be a divine creation, not a human achievement" (Hammett, 2007, p. 398). Hammett sees this motif developing in three ways throughout the whole of Scripture. By no coincidence, the motif develops along Trinitarian lines:

- God has made the promise: **I will be their God, and they will be my people.**
- The Holy Spirit is sent to dwell in the hearts of people. Fellowship is not found in the New Testament until the arrival of the Spirit at Pentecost.
- Christ's death is "the bringer of reconciliation and the

ultimate source of the church's unity and community" (Hammett, 2007, pp. 398-99).

Believers should pray that God will develop within their fellowship these principles so that they can enjoy the privilege of fellowship within the community of Christ. The love that is displayed in the communal relationships of the early Christian church has several distinct characteristics. Christian community involves love that is brotherly, free of judgment, humble, hospitable, not envious, forgiving, patient, honest, and kind. It involves the confession of and warning about sins, the carrying of burdens, a lack of grumbling, the presence of peace and mutual submission. Those who are in communion with Christ and His Church will also seek to encourage and comfort their fellow believers. The community of Christ is most importantly marked by the Gospel.

Biblical interpersonal relationships are marked by love. Love is the first mark of BIR (Long, 2004). Love is at the root of all the commands of God. As Jesus says in Mark 12 (quoting from Deuteronomy 6 and Leviticus 19):

> **'And you shall love the Lord your God with all your heart and with all your soul and with all your mind and with all your strength.' The second is this: 'You shall love your neighbor as yourself.' There is no other commandment greater than these.** (Mk 12:30-31 ESV)

He had been asked what the greatest commandment is. This was His reply. In fact, Matthew records that after giving this command, He said, **On these two commandments depend all the Law and the Prophets** (Mt 22:40 ESV). This love, however, is not superficial, as love so often is in contemporary society.

Love one another with brotherly affection. Outdo one another in showing honor (Rm 12:10), is foundational for Christian community. Paul here speaks of devotion and honor that is worked out in the love that Christians have for one another. This is not, however, just any type of devotion, but as Morris (1988) concludes, a devotion uniquely Christian. He reports the following about the word "brotherly love" (*philadelphia*):

> Unique to the Christians . . . the idea of brotherly love . . . is not found anywhere but among the Christians. They saw themselves as a family in a special sense. God was their Father and they were all brothers and sisters. Therefore they were united in a love that other people saw only in those of a natural family. (pp. 444-45)

With this in mind, Christians are, in reality, brothers and sisters, with the same Father and are commanded in Scripture to show affection as such. This love is vitally important for the spreading of the Gospel and the ministry of the church but does not always take place. Christian relationships should be as Harrison (1976) has said:

> To honor is to accord recognition and show appreciation. Presumably, this is based not on some attractiveness that is perceived or usefulness that is known but rather on the fact that every Christian has Christ in his heart and is able to express him through his own individuality...One honors God when he recognizes his transforming work in human life. (p. 132)

Brotherly love and the giving of honor go hand in hand and separate Christian relationships from those relationships found in the secular world.

Biblical interpersonal relationships are marked by withheld judgment and a lack of grumbling. The next mark of BIR found in the commandment not to judge others found in Romans 14:13:

> **Therefore let us not judge one another anymore, but rather determine this—not to put an obstacle or a stumbling block in a brother's way.**

There are differences between each Christian. No two believe exactly the same thing about every iota of theology. Paul, using the example of food, gives the command not to **judge one another anymore** or to **put an obstacle** in a fellow Christian's way. Often Christians refuse to have fellowship with other believers because they because they judge them for things that in reality are no different from the decision to eat all things or simply eat only vegetables (Rm 13:2).

R. Albert Mohler, Jr., in his book *The Disappearance of God* highlights issues that he rates as "first-order," "second-order," and "third-order" issues (Mohler, 2009, pp. 1-8). A good understanding of where various theological topics fit into these categories can rectify much of the tension between believers on issues that, in the end, should have little or no bearing on their ability to fellowship. Mohler says:

> First-level theological issues would include those doctrines most central and essential to the Christian faith. Included among these crucial doctrines would be doctrines such as the Trinity, the full deity and humanity of Jesus Christ, justification by faith and the authority of Scripture. (Mohler, 2009, p. 3)

These are non-negotiable and there is no biblical leeway to compromise on any of these points, therefore completely preventing genuine fellowship because they will result in "an eventual denial of Christianity itself" (Mohler, 2009, p. 5). "Second-order" issues, such as baptism, are those things which may be great enough to keep those on different ends of the argument from worshiping together on a regular basis, but do not prevent fellowship, as Mohler, a Southern Baptist, has clearly shown with his regular preaching in the Presbyterian church. Of the rest of theological issues, which Mohler calls "third-order," he writes:

> Christians may find themselves in disagreement over any number of issues related to the interpretation of difficult texts or the understanding of matters of common disagreement. Nevertheless, standing together on issues of more urgent importance, believers are able to accept one another without compromise when third-order issues are in question. (Mohler, 2009, p. 7)

This, however, is not always the case. Common examples include eschatology, Bible translations, and the music used in worship. Often there are disagreements, sometimes minute, which are dwelt upon to the extent that it becomes important for the Christian to alienate himself from anyone who does not have the same viewpoint he does. Here in Romans 14, Paul makes the case for fellowship for "second-order" and "third-order" issues. Here are men **for whom Christ died** (Rm 14:15), and they were being judged for what they ate. Paul saw bigger things at work and understood that believers should **pursue the things which make for peace and the building up of one another** (Rm 14:19).

This love is also demonstrated in the acceptance that must take place among believers. Paul gives the church at Rome the command to **bear the weaknesses of those without strength and not just please ourselves** (Rm 15:1). Christ has born the weakness of the lost and **did not please Himself** (Rm 15:3); therefore, the Christian should be accepting. This carries back into the discussion of judging above. Not only should the Christian not judge those who are within orthodoxy but have beliefs somewhat different from his own, the Christian is to be accepting of them. The believer must also be willing to bear weaknesses when she finds herself in a stronger position. This runs counter to everything that believers are told by contemporary culture. It runs against the accepted stream of Social Darwinism, which teaches that only the strong survive. Christians are in a race together. As Morris' quotes above so aptly puts, Christians are brothers and sisters. *Acceptance* here is not merely tolerance either. Christians do not simply tolerate one another. There may be tolerance of viewpoints, but the believer will find he is incapable of ministering as Christ has intended and laid forth in His Word, unless there is a genuine acceptance of other brothers and sisters in Christ. There must be a willingness to bear weaknesses and be of the same mind for Biblical community to take place (Rm 15:5).

Another passage tying into the idea of judgment in the Christian community is James 4:11: **Do not speak against one another, brethren. He who speaks against a brother or judges his brother, speaks against the law**... This is an easy sin to fall into, as it is easy to speak against another brother or sister on a number of different levels. How many conversations would not take place if there was an attitude present in which fellow believers were not talked against? James has been writing against misuse of the tongue and encouraging the brethren to avoid conflict. These two exhortations have a direct bearing on the context of his statement in verse eleven. Oftentimes, speaking against a brother or sister leads to even more sin against him or her and more importantly, against God. James has spoken of the effects of a small rudder on a large ship (Ja 3:4) and a small fire in a great forest (Ja 4:5); accordingly, seemingly small words have a large and lasting effect on the relationship between Christians. Davids (1989) writes:

> It is immaterial whether the accusations are true or false, for however true the charge may be, to spread it to people uninvolved in the situation is destructive to community harmony. **'Love covers a multitude of sins'** (1 Pet. 4:8). It does not broadcast sins, so Christians must not speak negatively about others. (p. 104)

Secondly, refraining from speaking against a fellow believer is a simple step in avoiding conflict. Words spoken against a brother or sister are often the beginning of conflict. Because the body of Christ is called as one family, conflict, in reality, is a splitting of the body. The efforts of the Church and of those in it are difficult enough without adding conflicts.

Adding to the mandate to withhold judgment and to avoid speaking against fellow Christians is a call to refrain from complaining. Fault is easy to find with others and James warns against complaining when he writes in James 5:9:

> **Do not complain, brethren, against one another, so that you yourselves may not be judged."** It is good to note that complaining is different from speaking against a brother or speaking evil. There are times when a complaint could be justified. However, in this context there is a clear indication that complaining is inferior because the focus of the Christian should be on his mission for Jesus. James has stated earlier that the time of God is near and a Christian should live in patient expectation. (Ja 5:7-8)

The relationship among believers should be characterized by a concentration on the high call of God—the Gospel. It is easy to get sidetracked into inferior matters, which often lead to sin and dis-fellowship. This is not in keeping with the commands and promises of Scripture. Calvin (1984) wrote, "[H]e [James] declares that thus they would all be condemned, because there is no one who does not offend his brethren, and afford them an occasion of groaning" (p. 249). Complaints do not accomplish anything for God's kingdom, but rather should be replaced with encouragement and godly correction.

Biblical interpersonal relationships are marked by peace. Peace must be present in Christian community. This comes, largely, through humility. No believer can say he loves his brothers and sisters when thinking too highly of himself. Galatians 5:26 gives this command as Paul writes, **Let us not become boastful, challenging one another, envying one another**. Paul is giving instructions for the Galatians to live by the Spirit (Gal 5:16) and in doing so, to put off the things of the flesh. Hendriksen (1968) summarizes this passage and comments on it:

> 'Let us neither brag about that which we have (or think we have), thereby calling forth equally pretentious swagger on the part of the person whom we are speaking, nor grudge that other person what he has.' Haughtiness and conceit, the 'know-it-all' attitude, brutal aggressiveness, these ill become those who claim to be followers of him who was always showing the very opposite spirit. ...God does not approve of windbags. If there had not been a special need for this warning Paul undoubtedly would not have issued it. (p. 227)

The Christian should not boast, challenging another believer to embrace the sin of envy. Likewise, he must not envy, causing arrogance in another. What Hendriksen places in parentheses is challenging as well. Most things which are bragged about either do not actually exist or are not the result of anything the believer has personally accomplished. Paul captures this sentiment in 1 Corinthians 3:6. He writes, **I planted, Apollos watered, but God was causing the growth.** Paul was obviously a great preacher and missionary, but he knew who always had the bragging rights—it is always Christ.

The Apostles knew well that peace was something gifted them from Christ Himself. As they say in the upper room three days after Christ's death peace was not something they were experiencing. Their Master, whom they had followed for several years, had been betrayed by one of their own number (Jn 18:1-9), arrested by the Romans (Jn 18:12), tried before the Jewish and Roman authorities (Jn 18:19-24; 28-40; 19:1-15), sentenced to death (Jn 19:16), nailed to a cross (Jn 19:18), died (Jn 19:30) and was buried (Jn 19:38-42). This left no peace.

They had deserted Jesus in the moment they should have stood boldly beside Him, just as Christ had said they would. (Jn16:32) They were followers of a man convicted of blasphemy (Jn 19:7) and they could have very well been the next ones nailed to a cross. They now find themselves on the first day of the week (Jn 20:19) and their turmoil has continued. The body of their Master is gone from the grave (Jn 20:2) and it is unclear to some of them what has happened. Has He risen? Has His body been stolen? And then the most unexpected thing occurs; that thing which He has promised all along. He appears to them as they sit in a locked room afraid of what is about to happen to them (Jn 20:19). Jesus comes and stands in their midst and says **Peace be with you**. Everything has changed in this moment. Not only is their Master there, in their midst, alive, but He *was* dead and is now alive.

Köstenberger (2004) comments on this passage that, "in Jesus' case, 'peace' was uniquely his gift to his followers by virtue of his vicarious sacrificial death on the cross. The expression may also function as a formula of revelation . . . Jesus' greeting was given to dispel any fears of his followers owing to their desertion prior to the crucifixion . . . This pertains particularly to Peter, who doubtless was in their midst as well" (p. 572). The disciples would not be able to carry out the mission that God already had for them if they did not have some type of peace.

For the Christian the *peace* that Christ offered to His disciples as He walked into that room is the same sustaining *peace* that provides the ability to carry out deep and meaningful relationships with other believers. *Peace* is not the ability provider, the gift of the Holy Spirit goes hand-in-hand with it; in truth the Holy Spirit is the provider of that *peace*. It is that *peace* that would have brought back to mind the words of Christ, in the time after His resurrection, to those disciples; words such as Jesus being the bread of life that gives eternal life (Jn 6:35-40) or the shepherd who takes care of His sheep (Jn 10:7-18). It was as He had been saying all along. The disciples had simply never grasped what it was He was talking about (Mk 9:32; Lk 9:45; Jn 12:16) but as John makes clear in his gospel, after Jesus is glorified they finally do understand (Jn 12:16). By grasping what has happened (something that still takes them several weeks to do) and by being able to experience *peace* through the sight of Jesus after His resurrection, they are now in the early stages of being prepared to take this message that He has instilled within them during His entire ministry.

Paul told the church at Rome, for the cause of Christ, life would be difficult and dangerous, **but in all these things we overwhelmingly conquer through Him who loved us.** (Rom 8:37) This truth should give the believer *peace* so that he is able to respond to the call of Christ to be in fellowship with other Christians.

Biblical interpersonal relationships are marked by a freedom from envy. Paul makes it clear that envy has no place in the Christian community. He gives clear instruction as he writes:

> **Godliness actually is a means of greater gain when accompanied by contentment. For we have brought nothing into the world, so we cannot take anything out of it either. If we have food and cover, with these we shall be content.** (1 Tm 6:6-8)

Christ's purpose for each Christian "is to glorify God and to enjoy him forever" (The Westminster Shorter Catechism). Within the church there have always been differences among believers. Some have great wealth, while others suffer impoverishment. Some will find employment, while others seek to no avail. There is, however, nothing to be envious of either way. **Love does not envy or boast; it is not arrogant** (1 Cor 13:4). The greatest confidence that Christians have is Christ and they have Christ in common with one another. This passage shows that there is nothing to brag about in any worldly situation. As Paul writes, **Let the one who boasts, boast in the Lord** (2 Cor 10:17).

Biblical interpersonal relationships are marked by forgiveness. Even if believers do put into practice, within their relationships, all those principles mentioned above, the reality is humanity is fallen and Christians still sin. Believers still wrong other people and, though they have forgiveness from Christ, they still sin in such ways as to need forgiveness from others. Forgiving hearts must be present in the Christian community. Paul writes:

> **So, as those who have been chosen of God, holy and beloved, put on a heart of compassion, kindness, humility, gentleness and patience; bearing with one**

another and forgiving each other, whoever has a complaint against anyone; just as the Lord forgave you, so also should you. (Col 3:12-13)

This passage in Colossians not only gives the command to forgive, but the reason. Paul spends the first seventeen verses of chapter three speaking of the new self that the Christian is to put on. This process of sanctification is preparing the believer for her eternal glorification, but does not eradicate sin in her life. This is why forgiveness must take place.

First, forgiveness must take place because of the new heart that God has given to His chosen, a heart of compassion, kindness, humility, gentleness and patience. This new heart is different from the heart of stone (Ez 36:26) and leads the Christian to react and live differently from the way he did when he was the old man (Rm 6:6). The new heart is full of love and should, therefore, display the characteristics of love (1 Cor 13:1-8).

Secondly, every person possesses a great debt that he personally owes to the Lord. This is a debt that he cannot pay, a debt which costs every human being his life (Rm 6:23) in both this life and the next (Rev 21:8). Jesus, however, has given mankind the opportunity to have his debt removed (Ps 103:12) and by suffering has made a way to God, for all people (1 Pt 3:18). The Christian has forgiveness (Eph 1:7; Col 1:14) but does not deserve it (Rm 5:8). Why then would there be any hesitation to forgive any brother or sister who has committed a wrong? King David writes in Psalm 51:4, **Against You, You only, I have sinned and done what is evil in Your sight.** D.A. Carson, in a sermon entitled "On Being Prepared for Suffering," points out that God is always the most offended party when sin takes place (Carson, 2005). Yet, though He is the most offended party when sin takes place, He is graciously willing to forgive. When a believer is wronged by another, she must realize that

God was the One most offended by her brother's sin. She should, therefore, have a much easier time forgiving than God did.

A Christian should not only forgive as God has forgiven, but with the same finality. Just as Psalm 103:12 tells believers that God removes transgressions **as far as the east is from the west**, so Christians too must forgive and move forward in Christian community. Continuing to act as if another brother still owes a debt is not the design of forgiveness for those in Christ.

Biblical interpersonal relationships are marked by patience. Patience is a difficult concept to grasp in contemporary culture. Twenty-first century society is on-demand and round-the-clock. From twenty-four hour news stations to never-closing grocery stores, there is little room for patience. But Paul, in Ephesians 4:1-2, calls for it when he writes, **Therefore I, a prisoner of the Lord, implore you to walk in a manner worthy of the calling with which you have been called, with all humility and gentleness, with patience, showing tolerance for one another in love.** Andrew T. Lincoln (1990) writes of this verse:

> μακροθυμία, 'patience,' is literally 'long temper' in contrast to a short temper and can have the sense of steadfastness or forbearance. Since relationships with others are in view, it is the latter sense that is relevant here... This ability to make allowance for others' shortcomings, this tolerance of others' exasperating behavior is a fruit of the Spirit (Gal 5:22) and again a quality essential for communal living. (p. 236)

Christians are not perfect, but not every shortcoming is a sin that needs forgiveness. Oftentimes simple patience will be sufficient for a relationship to move forward. Francis Foulkes (1989) writes, "*Patience (makrothymis)*, [is] a word...used...of slowness in avenging wrong or retaliating when hurt by another. It is used of God's patience with humanity . . . and the corresponding and consequent quality that the Christian should show towards others" (pp. 117-18). Biblical community is to be marked by patience between brothers and sisters in Christ. This community treats each other as equals, while keeping in mind that each member of the community is at a different place in his relationship with Christ and that patience is necessary for the health of the group. The community is also vividly aware of the patience that God has shown His people. They frequently draw to mind that **while we were still sinners, Christ died for us** (Rm 5:8).

Biblical interpersonal relationships are marked by honesty. Paul tells the church at Colossae, **Do not lie to one another, since you laid aside the old self with its evil practices** (Col 3:9). He has told them previously that they are to die to the old things and follow Christ (Col 3:3). One of the primary marks of the old self is lying, and in Christ, it has no place. Lying has no place in Christian community as well. Patzia (1990) writes, "Lying…certainly fits the context as a verbal sin as well as causing grievous damage to personal relationships, particularly within the body of Christ" (p. 74). Trust is hard enough to gain from someone. Lying destroys that trust and often ensures that it will never be gained back.

Lying was the first demonstration of what the sin nature, now present in every human, would look like. Lying began when the serpent informed Eve that if she ate of the tree in the middle of the garden that she **[S]urely will not die! For God knows that in the day you eat from it your eyes will be opened, and you will be like God, knowing good and evil** (Gn 3:4-5). Mankind's eyes were open to evil but closed to God. No longer could he commune with God in the cool of the evening. Rather he would hide when God walked in the Garden. Men would be cursed to toil the ground and women to struggle in childbirth. A lie started the downfall of man, his castigation from the Garden of Eden, and the punishment of death.

This drives point that the truth is important. Jesus said, **I am the way, the truth, and the life** (Jn 14:6). The truth must be a staple of Christian community. Obviously, the Truth, meaning Jesus, must be present, but also the words spoken among the believers must be honest words. This is difficult and sets Christian communion apart from the interpersonal relationships of the world. Honesty and truth are not valued by the unregenerate, but this must not be the case among believers. True Christian community will value the truth above all else.

Biblical interpersonal relationships are marked by kindness. The walk of those who are outside the body of Christ is in "futility of...mind (Eph 4:17). The walk for the Christian, in contrast, should be with a sound mind. A sound mind for the Christian comes through those actions laid out in part in Ephesians 4:32: **Be kind to one another, tender-hearted, forgiving each other, just as God in Christ also has forgiven you.** Paul has been discussing the needed unity among those who have faith in Christ (Eph 4:1-6). He now turns to the walk of the Christian. This passage speaks of being kind, and of forgiving (which has already been discussed). Kindness is not always considered a desirable trait for a human being to have, especially a man. There is a sense in which men are to be rugged and crass, though some seek now to swing the pendulum too far in the other direction and feminize men. This sentiment is depicted in many contemporary television shows where there is very little kindness shown. A popular movie, entitled *A Knight's Tale*, provides a good example to this fallacious attitude. One particular scene depicts a joust in which one knight allows another to finish without causing him further bodily harm, essentially allowing him to forfeit. The knight's love interest in the movie exclaims to a person also watching the joust that the knight "shows mercy." The onlooker quickly refutes this, stating, "He shows weakness" (Leder, Sewell, & Sossamon, 2002). That is the popular sentiment of much of culture.

This thinking, however, has no place in Christian community. A barrage of put-downs and insults, even though thought in jest, are, in reality, contrary to the speech that should take place among believers in Christ. William Hendriksen (1967) writes:

> *Kindness* is Spirit-imparted *goodness* of heart, the very opposite of the *malice* or *badness* mentioned in verse 31 [of Ephesians 4]. The early Christians by means of kindness commended themselves to others (II Cor. 6:6). God, too, is kind (Rom. 2:4; cf. 11:22). [And in Luke 6:25]…we are admonished to become like him in this respect. (p. 223)

A lack of kindness is very evident among young people, even in the church. They have grown up, for the most part, in a time that is desensitized to violence and anger. On television and in movies there are very few portrayals of people being kind to another person in their words and their actions. This makes for a difficult adjustment into a community that is called to kindness. Colossians 4:6 says, **Let your speech always be with grace, as though seasoned with salt, so that you will know how you should respond to each person.** The words and actions of the Christian community are to display Christ through their kindness.

***Biblical interpersonal relationships are marked by encouragement and comfort.* Encourage one another**. This phrase appears twice in Paul's first letter to the church at Thessalonica but the sentiments run throughout. Paul, in thinking about the fate of those who have died in Christ, has exhorted them to understand the power that Christ has over death. They will, **Always be with the Lord** (1 Thess 4:17). Bruce (1982) sees this command not in terms of something that is shallow or baseless but to the contrary, "The Thessalonian Christians are given solid grounds for comfort and hope" (p. 102). In 1 Thessalonians 5:11, Paul calls the Church to, **Encourage one another and build one another up.** They were not people of darkness, but lived in the light of Jesus Christ. The day was coming when Jesus would return and they were to be ready. Whether they were alive when He returned or whether they had "fallen asleep," they would have salvation in Christ.

The word used in both of these instances is *parakaleō*. Wells (1992) writes, "Strictly, it, means 'to call to one's side,' with the implication of giving aid, hence specifically, 'to urge' someone to action" (p. 58). Comfort and encouragement, therefore, aids in the discipleship process as believers are "built up" toward maturity. Holmes (1998) ties this back to the previously discussed term of *philadelphia.* He writes:

> Concerns about the fate of those who die before the Parousia and questions about its timing do not, for Paul, override the need to practice *phiadelphia*; to the contrary, they provide concrete occasions for its exercise, as believers comfort and encourage one another in the midst of difficult circumstances, confident in the hope of a salvation grounded in the death and resurrection of the Lord Jesus. (p. 169)

These two characteristics of biblical interpersonal relationships are vital as believers face adversity. In the world, Christians really depend only on each other.

Biblical interpersonal relationships are marked by submission. Ephesians 5:21 instructs believers to submit to one another, **Out of**

reverence for Christ. Obviously this is countercultural to contemporary society. Foulkes (1989) writes:

> In this verse there is an unexpected, but not illogical, turn in the apostle's exhortation, and one that leads him into the instructions that follow in the whole of the next section…He has implied…that the enthusiasm that the Spirit inspires is not to be expressed individualistically, but in fellowship. He has seen the dangers of individualism in a Christian community…He knew from experience that the secret of maintaining joyful fellowship in the community was the order and discipline that come from the willing submission of one person to another…Pride of position and the authoritarian spirit are destructive of fellowship. The importance to Paul of the whole concept of submission is evident from the use of the word more than twenty times in his letters…There must be a willingness in the Christian fellowship to serve any, to learn from any, to be corrected by any, regardless of age, sex, class, or any other division. (pp. 160-61)

There is true equality among believers in Christ (Rm 10:13). Patzia (1990) writes, "Fullness of Spirit leads to mutual subordination and unity, not to individual pride and disunity (p. 264; also Lincoln, 1990, p. 365). The submission envisioned by Paul is not, obviously, a lording over by authority. The key to the passage is not the submission itself, but that it is done in reverence to Christ. When believers are submitting in Christ there will be joy, just as there is with the singing of hymns (v. 19) and giving thanks to God the Father (v. 20).

Biblical interpersonal relationships are marked by hospitality. Grudem (1988) sees hospitality as a natural outgrowth of the Christian life. He writes of 1 Peter 4:9:

Earnest love, which seeks the good of others before one's own, finds practical expression in hospitality...[which] though a Christian duty, is to be offered *ungrudgingly to one another* without resenting the time and expense which may be involved...Such grumbling is ultimately a complaint against God and his ordering of our circumstances, and its result is to drive out faith, thanksgiving, and joy. Though hospitality to all people is certainly pleasing to God, Peter's emphasis on hospitality *to one another* – that is, to other Christians within the household of faith – is consistent with the rest of the New Testament. (p. 174)

The home of the Christian should be a welcoming and inviting place. The believer must put the needs of others above his own and seek the wellbeing of the fellow members of God's family. When Peter wrote, this exhortation also carried out practical implications. Kelly (1987) writes:

The lack of a network of decent hotels for ordinary people was one of the most striking social-economic differences between the ancient world and the modern, with the result that readiness to provide board and lodging for friends and other suitably sponsored travelers was even more highly esteemed that it is today. There was a great deal of coming and going in the early church...and in such a close-knit community it was natural that visitors should be put up by fellow-Christians. (pp. 178-79)

Jobes (2005) points out that this hospitality envisioned is not merely for travelers. It is to function, "Within and among the local community of believers" (p. 280). It would include opening homes for worship and fellowship. Jobes notes that this hospitality could become dangerous for the believer if they were in places where

Christians were persecuted. It was (and is) necessary for the church to function as commissioned.

Biblical interpersonal relationships are marked by the confession of sins and warning about sin. James tells his readers to confess their sins but not merely in some private prayer. He tells them to confess sins to each other. Davids (2002) writes that:

> The picture is that of a church gathering and the confession of sin to the assembled group. The mutual public confession (supplemented by private confession where public confession would not be appropriate) lays the basis for public prayer, in which people freed from all grudges, and resentments, and reconciled through confession and forgiveness, pray for healing for each other. (p. 124)

Confession of sins, like the other marks of biblical interpersonal relationships, serves to: "Help…as to God by the prayers of our brethren; for they know our necessities, are stimulated to pray that they may assist us; but they to whom our diseases are unknown are more tardy to bring us help" (Calvin, 1984, 358). Confession, therefore, is not seen as the opportunity for gossip and banter, but rather to make it possible for the carrying of burdens—another mark of biblical interpersonal relationships.

James makes it clear that warning others about their sin can save their souls from death (Jas 5:20). Paul writes in Colossians 3:16 that believers should admonish one another. This idea is easily coupled with that of the confession of sin. Believers are told to warn (admonish) other Christians about sin that is evident in their life. Many times the Christian has turned a blind eye to that sin and not until it is pointed out by another are the blinders removed. This is possible when Christians have strong meaningful relationships and, in turn, leads to stronger and deeper relationships.

Biblical interpersonal relationships are marked by the carrying of burdens. Jesus had demonstrated the greatest act of love in taking on the sin of the world when he was crucified on Golgotha. Paul reminds his readers in Galatians 6:2 that because of Christ's demonstration of love, they must bear the burdens of others if they are to fulfill the law of Christ. Paul's reasoning for using this phrase is unclear (Jervis, 1999). However, it is a pivotal moment as Paul redefines the, "Meaning of the law in light of Christ. Law now is that which is fulfilled through love (p. 154). Carrying burdens is, "Helping another Christian—sharing his load—whenever temptations oppress him or life depresses him" (Boice, 1976, p. 501).

George (1994) ferrets out three realties from this text that are important for believers to comprehend in their interpersonal relationships: (1) The reality of burdens, (2) the myth of self-sufficiency, and (3) the imperative of mutuality (pp. 413-14). Just because someone is in Christ does not mean they are without stress and burdens—the opposite is true. Christians who live in individualistic societies—like the one in America—must remember that it is impossible to be alone. As has previously been demonstrated, the call of Christ is a call to live in community. This shows that it is imperative to rely on others to flourish in one's faith in Christ. It is clear then that just as Jesus shouldered the burden of the cross as he walked toward His crucifixion, so believers are to shoulder the burdens of their fellow Christians.

The Gospel

A final attribute of Christian community is the centrality of the Gospel. This is the one attribute that no one outside of the body of Christ may claim. Some may argue they have love, or that they do not judge or have envy, but the Gospel is the great divide between saved and lost, believer and non-believer, elect and reprobate. All of the aforementioned characteristics of community are tied up in the Gospel. There is no greater love than the Gospel. There is no more superior nor definitive act of forgiveness than the forgiveness of the Gospel.

Believers in Christian community have the Gospel in their hearts and on their minds. There is a desire to allow the Gospel to define the actions of the community and have the Gospel at the center of those activities. This separates true Christian community from what often passes for fellowship in many churches. There should be a desire to let the wonderful relationships made possible through Christ point others toward a saving relationship with Him. Gilbert (2010) writes:

> I wonder if God's grace to you has caused you to love the world around you more, and to long to see people come to know and believe in Jesus Christ. If we truly understand the grace God has shown us, our hearts will burn to see that same grace shown to others. (p. 118)

The Christian community seeks to grow. Those who comprise it understand that they have been chosen by God for the purpose of bringing Him glory. They achieve this in great part by sharing with others the good news of what Christ has done. The Christian community is not a reclusive group. It is separated from the world because of the Gospel, but not out of the world. Members are called to the world to share with the world the Gospel (Jn 17:15-18).

It seems that for an extended period of ecclesiastical history, church was something you did as opposed to something you are. It also seems as if a new generation of believers has an intense desire to see church function as a community as opposed to an organization. Many young church leaders see the Christian community as a way of life as opposed to one of many activities that someone would plug into his calendar. This view must be present going forward. Harris (2004) writes:

> Passion for church involves diving into the community of the local church. It means 'doing life' with other Christians by pursuing relationships that extend beyond the church building and official church functions. . . . Fellowship means belonging to each other. . . . Every 'one another' command shows that the church isn't merely about programs or meeting, but about *shared life*. . . . The opportunity to share life with other Christians and experience this kind of fellowship is one of the most exciting parts of being a committed member of a local church. (pp. 75-77)

Along the same line of thinking, Stetzer (2003) writes:

> Community is a central value in most churches that are reaching postmoderns. Community will be a central value in all postmodern communities whether secular or sacred. This is good news for the church because community is central to its mission. With a culture anxious for genuine community, the church of Christ can offer community with man and with God. In the new church of the postmoderns, spiritual growth does not take place outside of community. (p. 150)

Community is God's design for the church. "You can't buy community; you can't program community" (Stetzer, 2003, p. 151). It is important for the church to recapture the community that is so prevalently seen in the Biblical record of the early church. They were a people on mission together in love and filled with the message of the Gospel. They were not perfect but they were together with all things in common (Acts 2:44). They were one, just as Jesus had prayed they would be (Jn 17:21). Biblical community in a contemporary Christian context must be marked by that same oneness for the sake of the Gospel of Christ.

The Effects of Social Media on Relationships

A recently launched website entitled *HeavenUp.com* was designed to draw Christians closer together. The founder of the website stated that, "My hope is that HeavenUp.com can be used as a resource to not only maintain and foster relationships with their local church and community but to grow spiritually and fellowship with people worldwide" (Koonse, 2012). The question then was asked, what does social media do to relationships? This has been asked even from the earliest days of the Internet's introduction into everyday life. Kraut et al. (1998) reflected back even before the existence of the internet and new technologies now taken for granted when they wrote:

> Since the introduction of computing into society, scholars and technologists have pondered its possible social impact. With its rapid evolution, large numbers of applications, wealth of information sources, and global reach to homes, the Internet has added even more uncertainty. People could use the Internet to further privatize entertainment (as they have purportedly done with television), to obtain previously inaccessible information, to increase their technical skills, and to conduct commercial transactions at home-each are somewhat asocial functions that would make it easier for people to be alone and to be independent. Alternatively, people could use the Internet for more social purposes, to communicate and socialize with colleagues, friends, and family through electronic mail and to join social groups through distribution lists, newsgroups, and MUDs. (p. 1018)

Christian and secular writers and researchers have been

interested in this effect since the advent of this new media. From a secular standpoint, the information is endless, but, in thinking about Christian relationships, the research is far from abundant.

Secular Research

In secular research there is no conclusive decision about social media. There are passionate voices and helpful research that come together in three differing perspectives of the impact of social media and the Internet on interpersonal relationships. Those perspectives are that social media is helping or having a positive impact, social media is transforming relationships into something other than what they previously were, or social media is hurting or having a negative impact (Hampton & Wellman, 2003).

Positive Perceptions. First, there are those who believe that social media specifically, and the Internet and new communications technologies in general, are having a positive effect on human's ability to connect on an interpersonal level. McKenna, Green, and Gleason (2002) found that the use of the Internet was improving and strengthening interpersonal relationships. They discovered that people were building relationships that were not only strong, but were lasting in the same manner as those that were not started in the online environment. They found that the, "Stability of relationships initially developed on-line compares favorably to that found in studies of relationships that had initially developed face to face" (p. 22). They conducted three separate studies that revealed participants who used the Internet frequently and who had developed relationships while doing so had a reduction in social anxiety, loneliness and depression. They write:

Study 1 showed that real, deep, and meaningful relationships do form on the Internet, and Study 2 found these relationships to be stable over time. Study 3 demonstrated that when people meet on the Internet, in the absence of gating features that are present in face-to-face situations, they like one another better than they would if they had initially met face to face. Further, this liking tends to survive a subsequent face-to-face encounter. (p. 28)

Their research was coupled with Kraut et al.'s (2002) as a rebuttal of their own previous work, Kraut et al. (1998) which showed an overall bleak picture of Internet use. McKenna and Green (2002) echoed much of their earlier work (McKenna, Green, and Gleason, 2002) which also stressing the helpfulness of the Internet in, "Creating new ties and to have membership in groups that would otherwise not be available to them" (124).

Bargh, McKenna, and Fitzsimons (2002) conducted three laboratory experiments to test the revelation of an individual's true-self to other Internet users. They write:

The present findings have identified two important and unique qualities of Internet (compared to face-to-face) communication: (1) that by its very nature, it facilitates the expression and effective commutation of one' true self to new acquaintances outside of one's established social network, which leads to forming relationships with them; and (2) that once those relationships are formed, features of Internet interaction facilitate the projection onto the partner of idealized qualities. (p. 45)

While point one is clearly a positive, Christian thought might put point two in the negative, as these idealized perception of others can, in the long term, be terribly detrimental to relationships. Bargh and McKenna (2004) reiterated their previous points on the positive aspects of social interaction on the Internet, while continuing to argue against any claim that the Internet, "Weaken[s] the fabric of neighborhoods and communities" (p. 585).

For Ellison, Steinfield, and Lampe (2007), the emphasis shifts from merely interaction on the Internet, to the use of social media. They are clear to distinguish between the two, stating:

> Online social network sites may play a role different from that described in early literature on virtual communities. Online interactions do not necessarily remove people from their offline world but may indeed be used to support relationships and keep people in contact, even when life changes move them away from each other. (p. 1165)

Though, obviously, there are risks with social media, the findings of the researchers: "demonstrate a robust connection between Facebook usage and indicators of social capital, especially the bridging type" (p. 1164). In their study of undergraduate students, they found that Facebook may actually have benefits for those users who have low self-esteem and low life satisfaction. Unlike research on the Internet before that showed the development of online relationships, this study showed that Facebook was being used to strengthen relationships that were already in existence offline.

Negative Perceptions. Kraut et al. (1998) conducted the first longitudinal study of the effect of the internet on the relationships of those who participated. For their study, participants who did not have the Internet were given a new computer and Internet access. They were given a pretest to ascertain their current well-being and subsequently post tested after 12 to 24 months. The researchers were able to view their online habits and the amount of time spent on web browsing and email composition. The researchers asked the participants about their social involvement and their psychological well-being. The researched showed:

> A surprisingly consistent picture of the consequences of using the Internet. Greater use of the Internet was associated with small, but statistically significant declines in social involvement as measured by communication within the family and the size of people's local social networks, and with increases in loneliness, a psychological state associated with social involvement. Greater use of the Internet was also associated with increases in depression. Other effects on the size of the distant social circle, social support, and stress did not reach standard significance levels but were consistently negative. (p. 1028)

The researchers had noted that where Putnam (1995) had already seen decline in the civic participation of Americans; the use of the internet exacerbated these declines.

Cummings, Butler, and Kraut (2000) studied students who used email in their communications with other people. The participants perceived email to be less useful than face-to-face meetings and telephone conversations for maintaining personal relationships. They did however see email as just as good for getting school work done and better than telephone or face-to-face interactions for the exchange of information.

Mesch (2001) examined Israeli adolescents, their activities, their internet use, and their perception of its effect on their relationships. He found that:

> In terms of leisure activities, frequent Internet users reported engaging more in outdoor activities, such as sports and going to movies, theater, singers' performances, and parties, than nonfrequent Internet users. But they also reported spending more time reading books…However, frequent Internet users

reported on average that they had fewer close friends and felt that the friends they had were less likely to listen to their problems…This finding is consistent with differences found in prosocial attitudes. Frequent Internet users reported on average that they placed less importance on helping others, understanding others, and contributing to society. (pp. 335-336)

Mesch also found that adolescents who had fewer friends that they considered to be close were more likely to be frequent Internet users.

Nie, Hillygus, and Erbring (2002) used a time diary study to find where there participants were spending their time. The researchers asked more than six thousand Americans about how they had spent their time in various blocks of time throughout the day. Their results saw that because of the Internet, respondents were spending less time with other human beings. They found that, "Internet use subtracts an additional 18 minutes a day, or almost an hour a week, in active participation with others at both work and play" (p. 224). This included time away from family, friends, and colleagues. The concluded that, "No matter how time online is measured, and no matter which type of social activity is considered, time spent on the Internet reduces time spent in face-to-face relationships, and concomitantly increase time spent alone" (pp. 225-27).

In an Australian study, Underwood and Findlay (2004) surveyed men and women who were in face-to-face relationships and also engaged in romantic relationships with someone through the Internet. These people were either married or in a committed relationships. Startling was the fact that most (76%) of the respondents did not believe that their Internet relationship was having an effect on their face-to-face relationship, although 38% had, "Met and had sex with their Internet partner [and] the remainder reported that their online relationship was sexual in nature" (p. 133-

34). Only 17% were engaged in a romantic relationship with someone online that was not sexual.

Mesch (2005) conducted a national study in Israel that reaffirmed his earlier work and was contrary to other work from the same time frame (see McKenna et al., 2002). He found that face-to-face relationships were viewed more highly than those developed online. Those who lived near each other were closer and had more trust in their friends. Respondents were more likely to view face-to-face friends as close friends. In contrast he observed that, "Adolescents with an online friend reported that this friend was known for a shorter time than face-to-face friends, they discussed fewer topics, and they participated in fewer shared activities" (p. 20). Overall, the study suggests that relationships that develop online are weaker than those that originate offline (p. 21).

Dwyer, Hiltz, and Passerini (2007) found that social media often does lead to the development of relationships but that the privacy on these sites is weak. Users may have perceived that they were able to trust these sites to safeguard their privacy, but that perception was inaccurate. The researchers reported that, "Online relationships can develop in sites where perceived trust is low and protection of privacy is minimal" (6).

Correa, Hinsley, and Zungia (2009) also distinguish social media research from previous research on Internet use. The anonymity once viewed as a distinguishing factor for the Internet over face-to-face interaction is gone (p. 252). They studied 959 cases selected at random to participate in their online survey. They tested for social media use, personality traits, life satisfaction, and socio-demographics. They found, in part, that the relationship between life satisfaction was negative and significant (p = .05) (p. 250). However, when emotional stability was taken into account, these differences disappeared (p. 252). This suggested, "That higher levels of anxiety were actually predicting social media use rather than level of person contentment with life" (p. 252).

Turkle (2011), who has been studying new technologies for more than thirty years, laments that the use of technology may be having a different outcome than its perceived effect:

> We are offered robots and a whole world of machine-mediated relationships on networked devices. As we instant message, email, text, and twitter, technology redraws the boundaries between intimacy and solitude. We talk of getting "rid" of our emails, as though these notes are so much excess baggage. Teenagers avoid making telephone calls, fearful that they will "reveal too much." They would rather text than talk. Adults, too, choose keyboards over the human voice. It is more efficient, they say. Things that happen in "real time" take too much time. Tethered to technology, we are shaken when that world "unplugged" does not signify, does not satisfy. After an evening of avatar-to-avatar life and, in the next, curiously isolated, in tenuous complicity with strangers. We build a following on Facebook or MySpace and wonder to what degree our followers are friends. We recreated ourselves as online personae and give ourselves new bodies, homes, jobs, and romances. Yet, suddenly, in the half-light of virtual community, we may feel utterly alone. As we distribute ourselves, we may abandon ourselves. Sometimes people experience no sense of having communicated after hours of connection. And they report feelings of closeness when they are paying little attention. In all of this, there is a nagging question: Does virtual intimacy degrade our experience of the other kind and indeed, of all encounters, of any kind? (pp. 11-12)

Turkle sees a trend of people connected but alone. She writes of a grandmother-granddaughter relationship that because of the great distances between them is most often experienced over Skype.

Because the granddaughter will often be working on other tasks while also speaking with her grandmother, Turkle observes that they "were more connected than they had ever been before, but at the same time, each was alone (p. 14).

No Effect. Anderson and Tracey (2001) studied adolescents in the United Kingdom during the early introduction of the Internet into the everyday life of the citizenry. They found:

> No evidence from this data that individuals who now have Internet access in their household (and who use it) are spending less time watching television, reading books, listening to the radio, or engaged in a social activities in the household in comparison with individuals who do not (or who no longer) have Internet access in their households. (p. 471)

This portion of their research, however, is not consistent with more recent studies (contra. Clough, 2000; Auday & Coleman, 2009; Haythronthwaite, 2001). Anderson and Tracey did find that those people who did gain access to the Internet were, overall, not willing to give up access completely.

Christian Research & Secular Research on Christian Relationships

Near the beginning of the commercialization of the Internet, there were those who looked at the phenomenon itself. They were not necessarily researching what effect the Internet and social communication media were having, but rather simply what was going on in this new form of communication. Bedell (1999) expounds on the sensation of the Internet based church. Moriarty (2005) examined the Christian social networking site, 5loaves.net.

One of the earliest researchers to study the Internet's effect on Christians was Clough (2000). He examined the danger posed by the Internet in promoting, "An overly individualistic world-view" (p. 99). At the time he wrote there were only forty million computers tied in to the web. Now there are more than 145 million people connected to the Internet (U.S. Census Bureau, 2010, Table 5). Clough reasoned that at that time it was still more likely for a child to mistakenly dial a sex chat line on a telephone than to stumble across pornographic material on the Internet. He was still skeptical of this new mediums benefit to Christians. While not taking an "apocalyptical" view of the Internet, he is cautious, writing:

> My thesis is the more modest one that Internet privileges a mistaken view of the relationship between the individual and community, and so will overall be a negative influence in the creation of strong communities and institutions. (p. 99)

He encouraged his readers to see that the Internet provided a task to the Church to:

> Draw attention to the benefits and costs the Internet will bring, and point to the way to a faithful and discerning use of this technology in the life of the Children of God. In the first place, we must recognize that the Internet may not be a benign or even neutral technology—this medium has its own message, a message that stands in opposition to the one we are called to proclaim. (p. 100)

Morris, Beck, and Smith (2004) examined the need for spiritual integration for the retention of students at Evangelical colleges. As is shown in the examination of Auday and Colman (2009), which is discussed below, students in Evangelical colleges spend large portions of their day engaged with social media. Therefore the authors call for Christian higher education to, "Find innovative ways to create a climate on campus where students can grow spiritually" most assuredly extends to their use of social medial.

Heinemann (2007) studied the interaction between teachers and students in online theological education. This is helpful because he discovered that the students surveyed had a more than satisfactory level of approval about the interaction with their teachers. For Heinemann, this is important because, "For teachers in theological education, adequate interaction with students would be a matter not only of best educational practice, but also of good theology" (p. 195).

Auday and Coleman (2009) studied the addictive nature of social media among Evangelical Christians. Their study found that more than half of respondents who used the social networking site Facebook reported they neglected "Important areas in their life due to spending too much time using the product" (p. 4). Some students saw their electronic devices as unwanted stressors and felt distracted from things that were actually important.

While there were reported negative effects, positives were also accentuated. More than forty percent believe that "It has helped alleviate stress in their lives" (p. 5). According to the research, about one in ten students believed that their time spent in electronic activities kept them from harmful or destructive activities (p. 5). Students indicated that they were glad to be able to connect with people who were geographically far away.

Most important to the study of Christian relationships were the respondents were asked about how networking activities were affecting social relationships:

> 35% reported that their time using networking activities has improved the quality of their social relationships, whereas only 25% believe that it has not (the remainder are "neutral").

The result that over one third of the students believe that social networking technology fosters relationships is interesting, particularly when one considers that over 35% agreed that their usage decreases time spent socializing face-to-face. One area that should be explored in the future is the long-term impact of managing relationships via social networking in comparison with those who are maintained through face-to-face encounters. (p. 5)

There seems to be, therefore, a mixed reaction on how students see social media effecting their lives. The authors of this study were gracious enough to provide this researcher with detailed information from their study about the perception of their respondents about various forms of social media's effect on their relationships. That information is included in the subsequent tables.

Table 1

Pulling off the Mask: Relationships suffered-MySpace

		Frequency	Percent	Valid Percent	Cumulative Percent
Valid	strongly disagree	1003	74.6	81.9	81.9
	disagree	76	5.7	6.2	88.2
	neutral	116	8.6	9.5	97.6
	agree	26	1.9	2.1	99.8
	strongly agree	3	.2	.2	100.0
	Total	1224	91.1	100.0	
Missing	System	120	8.9		
Total		1344	100.0		

Table 2

Pulling off the Mask: Relationships suffered-Facebook

		Frequency	Percent	Valid Percent	Cumulative Percent
Valid	strongly disagree	873	65.0	69.1	69.1
	disagree	223	16.6	17.6	86.7
	neutral	102	7.6	8.1	94.8
	agree	56	4.2	4.4	99.2
	strongly agree	10	.7	.8	100.0
	Total	1264	94.0	100.0	
Missing	System	80	6.0		
Total		1344	100.0		

Table 3

Pulling off the Mask: Relationships suffered-blogs

		Frequency	Percent	Valid Percent	Cumulative Percent
Valid	strongly disagree	1000	74.4	82.4	82.4
	disagree	75	5.6	6.2	88.6
	neutral	129	9.6	10.6	99.3
	agree	7	.5	.6	99.8
	strongly agree	2	.1	.2	100.0
	Total	1213	90.3	100.0	
Missing	System	131	9.7		
Total		1344	100.0		

Table 4

Pulling off the Mask: Relationships suffered-Twitter

		Frequency	Percent	Valid Percent	Cumulative Percent
	strongly disagree	1015	75.5	84.2	84.2
	disagree	35	2.6	2.9	87.1
Valid	neutral	155	11.5	12.9	99.9
	agree	1	.1	.1	100.0
	Total	1206	89.7	100.0	
Missing	System	138	10.3		
Total		1344	100.0		

Table 5

Pulling off the Mask: Relationships suffered-text messaging

	Frequency	Percent	Valid Percent	Cumulative Percent
strongly disagree	907	67.5	73.0	73.0
disagree	162	12.1	13.0	86.0
neutral	105	7.8	8.4	94.4
agree	63	4.7	5.1	99.5
strongly agree	6	.4	.5	100.0
Total	1243	92.5	100.0	
System	101	7.5		
Total	1344	100.0		

Table 6

Pulling off the Mask: Relationships suffered-instant messaging

		Frequency	Percent	Valid Percent	Cumulative Percent
Valid	strongly disagree	919	68.4	73.6	73.6
	disagree	135	10.0	10.8	84.4
	neutral	114	8.5	9.1	93.5
	agree	70	5.2	5.6	99.1
	strongly agree	11	.8	.9	100.0
	Total	1249	92.9	100.0	
Missing	System	95	7.1		
Total		1344	100.0		

Bobkowski and Kalyanaraman (2010) investigated the self-disclosure of Christians in online environments and its effect on the perception of others toward those Christians. They found that Christians who extensively disclosed that they were Christians were often judged as *more likeable* by both religious and non-religious respondents (p. 465). Overall, those people who extensively disclose through social media that they are Christians are likely to face, "Impressions [that] tend to be negative" (p. 465). It was also true that those who were the least religious found those who extensively disclosed that they were Christians to be less desirable, romantically. This is not necessarily bad or unexpected and the converse was true. Those respondents who were most religious found the extensively disclosing Christian both likeable and significantly more romantically desirable. This is important for Christian relationships because it shows that Christians are able to detect their own within social media platforms and are drawn to like-minded believers.

Challis (2011) asks his readers, presumably from the Church, if they understand what is going on. "We now consider community what was previously mere *communication*...Our perception of community is becoming disembodied, a product of mediated communication based on shared interest rather than a product of face-to-face communication based on shared space" (p. 103). Challis has concerns about what current technology is doing to the Church and Christians. It challenges, for instance, authority as defined in Scripture, taking it away from God and those who have been entrusted with His message, and gives it to anyone who can set up a blog or website. These realities demand that the Church explore what is happening when Christians step in to the virtual world of social media. Even more so, with the advent of churches that fully function online, it is necessary to know how participants in the Christian faith understand the media that has enveloped them.

3 RESEARCH DESIGN AND METHODOLOGY

The following chapter examines the research design and methodology for this study. This was a quantitative study that utilized a questionnaire to examine the perception of social media's effect on biblical interpersonal relationships. This questionnaire combined demographic data and Likert scale questions that asked participants to evaluate social media's effect on fifteen characteristics of their relationships with other Christians.

Research Purpose

Technology and social media have changed the way people communicate. In the major countries of the world, most people are using technology on a daily basis, with 85% using cell phones and 75% of those same people send text messages. At least 1 in 4 people in 15 of the world's largest countries use social media regularly. In the U.S., 73% of 18-29 year-olds use their cell phone to access the Internet (Pew, 2011). 66% of all Americans are using social media (Barna, 2008). Human beings seem to be more connected than ever.

However, is this "connection" real? Sherry Turkle (2011), noted MIT psychologist, who has studied new technologies for more than thirty years, laments that the use of technology may be having a different outcome than its perceived effect:

Christians are not immune from experiencing this new "connectedness." The Church already has an online presence. According to statistics from 2008, more than 6 in 10 Protestant churches have an online presence and more than half contact some large segment of their membership with email (Barna, 2008). Has this foray into the cyber world strengthened Christian relationships? Do Christians believe that they are closer and more connected to their fellow believers? What effect does that connectivity through social media have on interpersonal relationships? The answers to those questions are vital for believers to consider as more and more is done to connect people through the use of social media.

Tim Challis (2011), noted pastor and blogger, asks his readers, presumably from the Church if, they understand what is going on. "We now consider community what was previously mere *communication*...Our perception of community is becoming disembodied, a product of mediated communication based on shared interest rather than a product of face-to-face communication based on shared space" (p. 103). Challis has concerns about what current technology is doing to the Church and Christians. It challenges, for instance, authority as defined in Scripture, taking it away from God and those who have been entrusted with His message, and gives it to anyone who can set up a blog or website. These realities demand that the Church explore what is happening when Christians step in to the virtual world of social media. Even more so, with the advent of churches that fully function online, it is necessary to know how participants in the Christian faith understand the media that has enveloped them.

Therefore, because of the data available about who is consuming the most social media the purpose for this researcher was to discover if NACCSS perceive a positive or negative impact on their relationships through the use of social media. This study has begun to shed light on whether or not this subset of the Christian population is being affected by the ever-increasing use of social media. This researcher sought to help churches and Bible colleges assess where and how they can use social media to build strong BIRs in their particular settings.

Sampling

This study included 3,645 subjects from more than forty schools in the United States and Canada. Each school chose its own method of contacting their students with information about the availability of the questionnaire posted online at http://www.oneanotherproject.org.

While the researcher was unable to determine the exact number of students contacted, it was more than 20,000. The inability to determine the exact number was due to a number of schools who could not identify exactly how many students they contacted with the questionnaire information.

The researcher contacted more than two hundred schools to participate in the study. Forty schools agreed to participate explicitly. Fifty-nine (1.6%) of the subjects either indicated a school that did not agree to participate or gave an answer that did not allow them to be grouped with one of the participating schools. The subjects were purposefully gathered from schools that indicated that they were affiliated with a Christian denomination or were founded with historic Christian principles.

Each school determined how they best could contact their student body with information regarding the study. Schools were provided with a template email and were able to develop it to meet the needs of their medium of communication. Schools sent emails to their student body, published information for the study in their newsletter, and announced the study during chapel services.

Research Questions, Sub-Problems and Hypotheses

The following questions served as the basis for the development of the survey instrument, the collection of data and the subsequent analysis of the collected data:

- What, if any, is the positive relationship between social media use and biblical interpersonal relationships as perceived by North American Christian college and seminary students?

- What, if any, is the negative relationship between social media use and biblical interpersonal relationships as perceived by North American Christian college and seminary students?

- What is the perceived effect of social media use on biblical interpersonal relationships among North American Christian college and seminary students?

From the research questions, there arose eight sub-problems that taken together will make it possible to answer the research questions. They are:

- What, if any, is the relationship between time spent in church activities and the perception of the effect of social media use on biblical interpersonal relationships among North American Christian college and seminary students?

- What, if any, is the relationship between time spent using social media and the perception of the effect of social media use on biblical interpersonal relationships among North American Christian college and seminary students?

- What, if any, is the relationship between gender and the perception of the effect of social media use on biblical interpersonal relationships among North American Christian college and seminary students?

- What, if any, is the relationship between age and the perception of the effect of social media use on BIR among

North American Christian college and seminary students?

▪ What, if any, is the relationship between whether or not a subject has shared his/her faith through social media and the perception of the effect of social media use on biblical interpersonal relationships among North American Christian college and seminary students?

▪ What, if any, is the relationship between whether or not a subject has prayed with someone through social media and the perception of the effect of social media use on biblical interpersonal relationships among North American Christian college and seminary students?

▪ What, if any, is the relationship between class rank and the perception of the effect of social media use on biblical interpersonal relationships among North American Christian college and seminary students?

▪ What, if any, is the relationship between the used by a student for classes and the perception of the effect of social media use on biblical interpersonal relationships among North American Christian college and seminary students?

Research Procedures

The questionnaire used for this study was designed in two parts. The first gathered demographic data which the researcher used to divide the respondents in to groups so that conclusions could be drawn about what variables were affecting the answers given by the respondents. These demographic questions were necessary to satisfy the research questions and sub-problems.

Second, respondents were asked to rank on a Likert scale their perceptions on social media's effect on fifteen areas identified as essential to biblical interpersonal relationships. The researcher, through the review of the literature presented in chapter two, developed fifteen characteristics of biblical interpersonal relationships as presented in Scripture. These characteristics were developed into a Likert scale enquiring of the subjects their perception of the effect of social media on these characteristics.

To gather the needed data for this study, the researcher contacted more than two hundred self-described Christian colleges and seminaries across the United States and Canada. These schools were asked to participate in the study by sending out a link to the researcher's questionnaire. Forty schools participated in the study and 3,645 questionnaires were collected.

The survey was posted at http://www.oneanotherproject.org and respondents were able to access this website at their leisure. Each school chose to send out the link in the way in which they believed would best reach their students. The schools were provided with a template email that they could format into whatever medium best suited their needs.

The data was then examined using IBM's SPSS Statistics 20. The means of results from the Likert scale questions were compared with the demographic information gathered from the respondents. These comparisons led to the results reported in *Chapter Four*.

Number and Characteristics of Participants

This study involved NACCSS from across the United States and Canada. The total number of questionnaires collected was 3,645. The students ranged in age from 17 to over 60 years old and included undergraduate, graduate, and doctoral students. In addition, both online and on campus students were surveyed about the their social media use.

This population was important because they encounter new technology every day. They will be more inundated with new technology than any generation before them. Secular science is showing that this technology has an enormous effect on how humans interact. Interaction, or community, is a valued in Christianity. It is a part of God's design for man. Therefore, to see how students understood the effect of social media was invaluable.

Process of Research and Timelines

The researcher, through extensive internet database searches, contacted more than 200 Bible Colleges, Christian schools, and seminaries during the spring semester of 2012. Each school was contact through their president or his designee. Those schools that agreed to participate were given a template email with which to contact their student body. These emails began being sent on March 23, 2012. The first questionnaire was completed on March 23, 2012 and the final one finished July 2, 2012.

4 RESULTS

This study involved NACCSS from across the United States and Canada. The total number of questionnaires collected was 3,645. The students ranged in age from 17 to over 60 years old and included undergraduate, graduate, and doctoral students. In addition, both online and on campus students were surveyed about their social media use. In this chapter, the results are presented and considered in light of the research questions, sub-problems and the hypotheses.

The first section of this chapter presents the overall results of the study. These are presented in frequency tables. The second section of the chapter considers the results of the three research questions. The third and final section of this chapter examines the eight sub-problems and compares the means of these eight variables to determine where significant differences existed between the various demographic variables.

First, there were forty colleges, universities, and seminaries that participated in some official capacity. The *undefined* field includes 59 (1.6%) respondents who indicated a school that had not officially agreed to participate. It is not known how they came to take the survey, but it was publicly available, though not publicly advertised. It may be that they were encouraged to participate by someone with knowledge of the study.

Demographic Data

Table 7

School	Frequency	Percent	Cumulative Percent	
Acadia Divinity School	1	.0	.0	
Allegheny Wesleyan College	6	.2	.2	
Andover Newton Theological School	14	.4	.6	
Baptist Bible College	217	6.0	6.5	
Baptist University of the Americas	15	.4	6.9	
Belhaven University	96	2.6	9.6	
Biola University	6	.2	9.7	
Brookes Bible Institute	4	.1	9.8	
Canadian Southern Baptist Seminary and College	16	.4	10.3	
Charleston Southern	196	5.4	15.7	
College of Biblical Studies	23	.6	15.7	100.0
Columbia Evangelical Seminary	4	.1	15.8	
Columbia International University	193	5.3	21.1	
Crossroads Bible College	12	.3	21.4	
Dallas Christian College	30	.8	22.2	
Eston College	22	.6	22.8	
Florida Christian College	11	.3	23.1	
Golden Gate Baptist Theological Seminary	113	3.1	26.2	
Greenville College	290	8.0	34.2	
Guido Bible Institute	5	.1	34.3	
Hannibal La-Grange University	100	2.7	37.1	

Table 8

School	Frequency	Percent	Cumulative Percent
Johnson University	66	1.8	38.9
Master's College and Seminary	59	1.6	40.5
Midwestern Baptist Theological Seminary	171	4.7	45.2
Mississippi College	20	.5	45.7
Montreat College	50	1.4	47.1
New Hope Christian College	73	2.0	49.1
New Orleans Baptist Theological Seminary	34	.9	50.0
North Greenville University	143	3.9	54.0
Oklahoma Baptist University	223	6.1	60.1
Prairie Bible Institute	52	1.4	61.5
Rocky Mountain College	9	.2	61.8
Southeastern Baptist Theological Seminary	498	13.7	75.4
Southwestern Baptist Theological Seminary	188	5.2	80.6
Spring Arbor University	209	5.7	86.3
Taylor College and Seminary	51	1.4	87.7
The Master's College	151	4.1	91.9
Toccoa Falls College	105	2.9	94.7
Valley Forge Christian College	110	3.0	97.8
Undefined	59	1.6	99.4
Total	3645	100.0	

Table 9

Do you consider yourself a Christian?

	Frequency	Percent	Valid Percent	Cumulative Percent
Yes	3608	99.0	99.0	99.0
No	37	1.0	1.0	100.0
Total	3645	100.0	100.0	

Nearly all (99.0%) of those students who participated in the study indicated that they considered themselves Christians. Those who indicated they did not consider themselves to be Christians were not included in the analysis of the data.

Table 10

What is your gender?

	Frequency	Percent	Valid Percent	Cumulative Percent
Male	1658	45.5	45.5	45.5
Female	1987	54.5	54.5	100.0
Total	3645	100.0	100.0	

Of those studied, the majority (54.5%) were female. The rest of the students (45.4) indicated they were males.

Table 11

In what format do you take classes?

	Frequency	Percent	Valid Percent	Cumulative Percent
On Campus	3184	87.4	87.4	87.4
Online/Distance Learning	461	12.6	12.6	100.0
Total	3645	100.0	100.0	

The majority of students (87.4%) who responded indicated that they took classes in traditional seated format on campus. The remaining students (12.6%) were engaged in coursework administered through online/distance learning.

Table 12

What is your class rank?

	Frequency	Percent	Valid Percent	Cumulative Percent
Freshman	570	15.6	15.6	15.6
Sophomore	607	16.7	16.7	32.3
Junior	647	17.8	17.8	50.0
Senior	663	18.2	18.2	68.2
Graduate Student	989	27.1	27.1	95.4
Doctoral Student	169	4.6	4.6	100.0
Total	3645	100.0	100.0	

The largest group of students (27.1%) were graduate students. However, when combined (68.2%), the vast majority of students were studying in undergraduate programs, ranking themselves as freshman (15.6%), sophomores (16.7%), juniors (17.8%), and seniors (18.2%). The remaining students (4.6%) indicated they work working in a doctoral program.

Table 13

About how many hours a week do you spend in activities organized by your local church?

	Frequency	Percent	Valid Percent	Cumulative Percent
Less than 1	582	16.0	16.0	16.0
1-3	1444	39.6	39.6	55.6
4-7	1024	28.1	28.1	83.7
8-12	325	8.9	8.9	92.6
13-20	93	2.6	2.6	95.1
More than 20	177	4.9	4.9	100.0
Total	3645	100.0	100.0	

The largest portion (39.6%) of students indicated that they spend 1-3 hours per week in activities organized by the local church. Combined, more than two-thirds of respondents (67.7%) spent between one and seven hours per week. The remaining students either spend less than one hour (16.0%), 13-20 hours (2.6%), or more than 20 hours (4.9%).

Table 14

About how many hours a week do you spend using social media?

	Frequency	Percent	Valid Percent	Cumulative Percent
Less than 1	194	5.3	5.3	5.3
1-3	774	21.2	21.3	26.6
4-7	1149	31.5	31.6	58.3
8-12	820	22.5	22.6	80.8
13-20	390	10.7	10.7	91.6
More than 20	306	8.4	8.4	100.0
Total	3633	99.7	100.0	
Missing	12	.3		
Total	3645	100.0		

The largest portion (31.5%) of students indicated that they spend 4-7 hours per week social media activities. Combined, more than half of respondents (54%) spent between 4 and 12 hours per week. The remaining students either spend less than one hour (5.3%), 1-3 (21.2%), 13-20 hours (10.7%), or more than 20 hours (8.4%).

Table 15

Please check all of these you own:

| | Cases | | | | | |
| | Valid | | Missing | | Total | |
	N	Percent	N	Percent	N	Percent
PC	2516	69.0%	1129	31.0%	3645	100.0%
MAC	1220	33.5%	2425	66.5%	3645	100.0%
Tablet	638	17.5%	3007	82.5%	3645	100.0%
Smart Phone	1767	48.5%	1878	51.5%	3645	100.0%

The majority of students (69.0%) who responded indicated that they owned a PC. Nearly half (48.5%) indicated they owned a smart phone. Just over one-third (33.5%) stated they owned a MAC and slightly less than one-in-five (17.5%) indicated they owned a tablet.

Table 16

Have you ever shared your faith through social media?

	Frequency	Percent	Valid Percent	Cumulative Percent
Yes	3017	82.8	82.8	82.8
No	628	17.2	17.2	100.0
Total	3645	100.0	100.0	

The vast majority (82.8%) of respondents indicated they had used social media to share their faith. A small minority (17.2%) of the students indicated they had not used social media to share their faith.

Table 17

Have you ever prayed with someone through social media?

		Frequency	Percent	Valid Percent	Cumulative Percent
	Yes	2205	60.5	60.8	60.8
Valid	No	1423	39.0	39.2	100.0
	Total	3628	99.5	100.0	
Missing	System	17	.5		
Total		3645	100.0		

A little over half (60.5%) of the students who responded to the survey indicated that they had prayed with another person through social media. However, there were many (39.0%) who indicated they had not done so. There were also a small number (.5%) who did not respond to this question.

Table 18

What effect does social media have on your ability to love other Christians?

	Frequency	Percent	Valid Percent	Percent
n/a	78	2.1	2.1	2.1
Negative	31	.9	.9	3.0
Somewhat Negative	256	7.0	7.0	10.0
No Effect	811	22.2	22.2	32.3
Somewhat Positive	1356	37.2	37.2	69.5
Positive	1113	30.5	30.5	100.0
Total	3645	100.0	100.0	

The largest portion of respondents (37.2%) indicated that they believed social media has a somewhat positive effect on their ability to love other Christians. Combined, a majority of respondents (67.7%) had a positive or a somewhat positive view of the effect of social media on their ability to love other Christians. The remaining students either had a negative view (.9%), somewhat negative (7.0%), or they felt it had not effect at all (22.2%). A fraction of the respondents (2.1%) chose to indicate they had no opinion.

Table 19

What effect does social media have on your ability to encourage other Christians?

	Frequency	Percent	Valid Percent	Cumulative Percent
n/a	94	2.6	2.6	2.6
Negative	15	.4	.4	3.0
Somewhat Negative	56	1.5	1.5	4.5
No Effect	264	7.2	7.2	11.8
Somewhat Positive	1114	30.6	30.6	42.3
Positive	2102	57.7	57.7	100.0
Total	3645	100.0	100.0	

The largest portion of respondents (57.7%) indicated that they believed social media has a positive effect on their ability to encourage other Christians. Combined, a majority of respondents (88.3%) had a positive or a somewhat positive view of the effect of social media on their ability to encourage other Christians. The remaining students either had a negative view (.4%), somewhat negative (1.5%), or they felt it had not effect at all (7.2%). A fraction of the respondents (2.6%) chose to indicate they had no opinion.

Table 20

What effect does social media have on your ability to be patient with other Christians?

	Frequency	Percent	Valid Percent	Cumulative Percent
n/a	77	2.1	2.1	2.1
Negative	125	3.4	3.4	5.5
Somewhat Negative	903	24.8	24.8	30.3
No Effect	1225	33.6	33.6	63.9
Somewhat Positive	865	23.7	23.7	87.7
Positive	450	12.3	12.3	100.0
Total	3645	100.0	100.0	

The largest portion of respondents (33.2%) indicated that they believed social media has no effect on their ability to be patient with other Christians. The next largest group (24.8%) indicated a somewhat negative view of social medias effect on their ability to be patient with other Christians. The remaining students indicated either a somewhat positive view (23.7%), a positive view (12.3%), or a negative view (3.4%). A fraction of the respondents (2.1%) chose to indicate they had no opinion.

Table 21

What effect does social media have on your ability to forgive other Christians?

	Frequency	Percent	Valid Percent	Cumulative Percent
n/a	134	3.7	3.7	3.7
Negative	68	1.9	1.9	5.5
Somewhat Negative	482	13.2	13.2	18.8
No Effect	1698	46.6	46.6	65.3
Somewhat Positive	822	22.6	22.6	87.9
Positive	441	12.1	12.1	100.0
Total	3645	100.0	100.0	

The largest portion of respondents (46.6%) indicated that they believed social media has no effect on their ability to forgive other Christians. The next largest group (22.6%) indicated a somewhat positive view of social media's effect on their ability to forgive other Christians. The remaining students indicated either a somewhat negative view (13.2%), a positive view (12.1%), or a negative view (1.9%). A fraction of the respondents (3.7%) chose to indicate they had no opinion.

Table 22

What effect does social media have on your ability to comfort other Christians?

	Frequency	Percent	Valid Percent	Cumulative Percent
n/a	71	1.9	1.9	1.9
Negative	28	.8	.8	2.7
Somewhat Negative	105	2.9	2.9	5.6
No Effect	388	10.6	10.6	16.2
Somewhat Positive	1405	38.5	38.5	54.8
Positive	1648	45.2	45.2	100.0
Total	3645	100.0	100.0	

The largest portion of respondents (45.2%) indicated that they believed social media has a positive effect on their ability to comfort other Christians. Combined, a majority of respondents (83.7%) had a positive or a somewhat positive view of the effect of social media on their ability to comfort other Christians. The remaining students either had a negative view (.8%), somewhat negative (2.9%), or they felt it had not effect at all (10.6%). A fraction of the respondents (1.9%) chose to indicate they had no opinion.

Table 23

What effect does social media have on your ability to submit to other Christians?

	Frequency	Percent	Valid Percent	Cumulative Percent
n/a	199	5.5	5.5	5.5
Negative	73	2.0	2.0	7.5
Somewhat Negative	408	11.2	11.2	18.7
No Effect	1901	52.2	52.2	70.8
Somewhat Positive	745	20.4	20.4	91.2
Positive	319	8.8	8.8	100.0
Total	3645	100.0	100.0	

A majority of respondents (52.2%) indicated that they believed social media has no effect on their ability to submit to other Christians. The next largest group (20.4%) indicated a somewhat positive view of social media's effect on their ability to submit to other Christians. The remaining students indicated either a somewhat negative view (11.2%), a positive view (8.8%), or a negative view (2.0%). A fraction of the respondents (5.5%) chose to indicate they had no opinion.

Table 24

What effect does social media have on your ability not to be prideful toward other Christians?

	Frequency	Percent	Valid Percent	Cumulative Percent
n/a	121	3.3	3.3	3.3
Negative	218	6.0	6.0	9.3
Somewhat Negative	1141	31.3	31.3	40.6
No Effect	1402	38.5	38.5	79.1
Somewhat Positive	503	13.8	13.8	92.9
Positive	260	7.1	7.1	100.0
Total	3645	100.0	100.0	

The largest portion of respondents (38.5%) indicated that they believed social media has no effect on their ability not to be prideful toward other Christians. The next largest group (31.3%) indicated a somewhat negative view of social media's effect on their ability not to be prideful toward other Christians. The remaining students indicated either a somewhat positive view (13.8%), a positive view (7.1%), or a negative view (6.0%). A fraction of the respondents (3.3%) chose to indicate they had no opinion.

Table 25

What effect does social media have on your ability to be at peace with other Christians?

	Frequency	Percent	Valid Percent	Cumulative Percent
n/a	90	2.5	2.5	2.5
Negative	84	2.3	2.3	4.8
Somewhat Negative	612	16.8	16.8	21.6
No Effect	1268	34.8	34.8	56.4
Somewhat Positive	1040	28.5	28.5	84.9
Positive	551	15.1	15.1	100.0
Total	3645	100.0	100.0	

The largest portion of respondents (34.8%) indicated that they believed social media has no effect on their ability to be at peace with other Christians. The next largest group (28.5%) indicated a somewhat positive view of social media's effect on their ability to submit to other Christians. The remaining students indicated either a somewhat negative view (16.8%), a positive view (15.1%), or a negative view (2.3%). A fraction of the respondents (2.5%) chose to indicate they had no opinion.

Table 26

What effect does social media have on your ability to show kindness to other Christians?

	Frequency	Percent	Valid Percent	Cumulative Percent
n/a	57	1.6	1.6	1.6
Negative	28	.8	.8	2.3
Somewhat Negative	161	4.4	4.4	6.7
No Effect	578	15.9	15.9	22.6
Somewhat Positive	1383	37.9	37.9	60.5
Positive	1438	39.5	39.5	100.0
Total	3645	100.0	100.0	

The largest portion of respondents (39.5%) indicated that they believed social media has a positive effect on their ability to show kindness to other Christians. Combined, a majority of respondents (77.4%) had a positive or a somewhat positive view of the effect of social media on their ability to comfort other Christians. The remaining students either had a negative view (.8%), somewhat negative (4.4%), or they felt it had not effect at all (15.9%). A fraction of the respondents (1.6%) chose to indicate they had no opinion.

Table 27

What effect does social media have on your ability to withhold judgment from other Christians?

	Frequency	Percent	Valid Percent	Cumulative Percent
n/a	94	2.6	2.6	2.6
Negative	434	11.9	11.9	14.5
Somewhat Negative	1527	41.9	41.9	56.4
No Effect	937	25.7	25.7	82.1
Somewhat Positive	425	11.7	11.7	93.7
Positive	228	6.3	6.3	100.0
Total	3645	100.0	100.0	

The largest portion of respondents (41.9%) indicated that they believed social media has a negative effect on their ability to withhold judgment from other Christians. Combined, majority of respondents (53.8%) had a negative or a somewhat negative view of the effect of social media on their ability to withhold judgment from other Christians. The remaining students either had a positive view (6.3%), somewhat positive (11.3%), or they felt it had not effect at all (25.7%). A fraction of the respondents (2.6%) chose to indicate they had no opinion.

Table 28

What effect does social media have on your ability not to grumble against other Christians?

	Frequency	Percent	Valid Percent	Cumulative Percent
n/a	123	3.4	3.4	3.4
Negative	341	9.4	9.4	12.7
Somewhat Negative	1368	37.5	37.5	50.3
No Effect	1177	32.3	32.3	82.6
Somewhat Positive	408	11.2	11.2	93.7
Positive	228	6.3	6.3	100.0
Total	3645	100.0	100.0	

The largest portion of respondents (37.5%) indicated that they believed social media has a somewhat negative effect on their ability not to grumble against other Christians. The next largest group (32.3%) indicated they believed social media had no effect on their ability to not to grumble against other Christians. The remaining students either had a positive view (6.3%), somewhat positive (11.2%), or they held a negative view (9.4%). A fraction of the respondents (3.4%) chose to indicate they had no opinion.

Table 29

What effect does social media have on your ability to be hospitable to other Christians?

	Frequency	Percent	Valid Percent	Cumulative Percent
n/a	107	2.9	2.9	2.9
Negative	46	1.3	1.3	4.2
Somewhat Negative	230	6.3	6.3	10.5
No Effect	1029	28.2	28.2	38.7
Somewhat Positive	1273	34.9	34.9	73.7
Positive	960	26.3	26.3	100.0
Total	3645	100.0	100.0	

The largest portion of respondents (34.9%) indicated that they believed social media has a somewhat positive effect on their ability to be hospitable to other Christians. Combined, majority of respondents (61.2%) had a positive or a somewhat positive view of the effect of social media on their ability to be hospitable to other Christians. The remaining students either had a negative view (1.3%), somewhat negative (6.3%), or they felt it had not effect at all (28.2%). A fraction of the respondents (2.9%) chose to indicate they had no opinion.

Table 30

What effect does social media have on your ability to confess your sins to other Christians?

	Frequency	Percent	Valid Percent	Cumulative Percent
n/a	169	4.6	4.6	4.6
Negative	194	5.3	5.3	10.0
Somewhat Negative	342	9.4	9.4	19.3
No Effect	1634	44.8	44.8	64.2
Somewhat Positive	908	24.9	24.9	89.1
Positive	398	10.9	10.9	100.0
Total	3645	100.0	100.0	

The largest portion of respondents (44.8%) indicated that they believed social media has no effect on their ability to confess your sins to other Christians. The next largest group (24.9%) indicated a somewhat positive view of social media's effect on their ability to confess your sins to other Christians. The remaining students indicated either a somewhat negative view (9.4%), a positive view (10.9%), or a negative view (5.3%). A fraction of the respondents (4.6%) chose to indicate they had no opinion.

Table 31

What effect does social media have on your ability to carry the burdens of other Christians?

	Frequency	Percent	Valid Percent	Cumulative Percent
n/a	88	2.4	2.4	2.4
Negative	48	1.3	1.3	3.7
Somewhat Negative	211	5.8	5.8	9.5
No Effect	735	20.2	20.2	29.7
Somewhat Positive	1462	40.1	40.1	69.8
Positive	1101	30.2	30.2	100.0
Total	3645	100.0	100.0	

The largest portion of respondents (40.1%) indicated that they believed social media has a somewhat positive effect on their ability to carry the burdens of other Christians. Combined, majority of respondents (70.3%) had a positive or a somewhat positive view of the effect of social media on their ability to carry the burdens of other Christians. The remaining students either had a negative view (1.3%), somewhat negative (5.8%), or they felt it had not effect at all (20.2%). A fraction of the respondents (2.4%) chose to indicate they had no opinion.

Table 32

What effect does social media have on your ability to warn other Christians about their wrong behaviors?

	Frequency	Percent	Valid Percent	Cumulative Percent
n/a	125	3.4	3.4	3.4
Negative	113	3.1	3.1	6.5
Somewhat Negative	380	10.4	10.4	17.0
No Effect	1024	28.1	28.1	45.0
Somewhat Positive	1385	38.0	38.0	83.0
Positive	618	17.0	17.0	100.0
Total	3645	100.0	100.0	

The largest portion of respondents (38.0%) indicated that they believed social media has a somewhat positive effect on their ability to warn other Christians about wrong behaviors. Combined, majority of respondents (55.0%) had a positive or a somewhat positive view of the effect of social media on their ability warn other Christians about wrong behaviors. The remaining students either had a negative view (3.1%), somewhat negative (10.4%), or they felt it had not effect at all (28.1%). A fraction of the respondents (3.1%) chose to indicate they had no opinion.

Table 33

Do you have an account on a social networking website (like Facebook or Myspace)?

		Frequency	Percent	Valid Percent	Cumulative Percent
	Yes	3389	93.0	93.1	93.1
Valid	No	252	6.9	6.9	100.0
	Total	3641	99.9	100.0	
Missing	System	4	.1		
Total		3645	100.0		

The vast majority (93.0%) of respondents indicated they had an account on a social networking website. A small minority (6.9%) of the students indicated they did not have an account on a social media website. A fraction of the respondents (.1%) chose to indicate they had no opinion.

Table 34

About how many of your "friends" on Facebook have you met in person?

		Frequency	Percent	Valid Percent	Cumulative Percent
Valid	All of them	1593	43.7	44.9	44.9
	Most of them	1680	46.1	47.4	92.4
	About half of them	135	3.7	3.8	96.2
	A few of them	43	1.2	1.2	97.4
	None of them	93	2.6	2.6	100.0
	Total	3544	97.2	100.0	
Missing	System	101	2.8		
Total		3645	100.0		

The largest portion of respondents (46.1%) indicated that they had met most of the people with whom they were "friends" on Facebook. Combined, majority of respondents (89.8%) indicated that they had met most of the people with whom they were "friends" on Facebook. The remaining students either had met about half of them (3.7%), a few of them (1.2%), or none of them (2.6%) A fraction of the respondents (2.8%) chose to indicate they had no opinion.

Results and the Research Questions

The second section of this chapter examines the results and how they answer the research questions. The overall means of each variable is considered to see which (1) which variables were considered positive, (2) which variables were considered negative, and (3) the overall view of social media's effect on the biblical interpersonal relationships as perceived by North American Christian college and seminary students.

Research Question One. The first research question was, "What, if any, is the positive relationship between social media use and biblical interpersonal relationships as perceived by North American Christian college and seminary students?"

This question is examined by looking at each of the fifteen "one another sayings" Likert scale. An answer of negative was scored as a (1), somewhat negative was scored as a (2), no effect was scored as a (3), somewhat positive as a (4), and positive was scored as a Means over 3.00 indicate a positive overall perception of this characteristic of BIR.

Twelve of the questions with a Likert scale had means that were larger than 3.00 indicating that the subjects believed that social media was having a more positive effect on their BIR. The ability to encourage, comfort, and show kindness rated above positive (4.00). These results are available in Table 35.

Table 35

Positive Perceptions

	Valid	Missing	M
Encourage	**3551**	**94**	**4.4734**
Comfort	**3574**	**71**	**4.2703**
Kindness	**3588**	**57**	**4.1265**
Carry burdens	**3557**	**88**	**3.9438**
Love	**3567**	**78**	**3.9151**
Hospitable	**3538**	**107**	**3.8115**
Warn	**3520**	**125**	**3.5724**
Peace	**3555**	**90**	**3.3831**
Forgive	**3511**	**134**	**3.3093**
Confess sins	**3476**	**169**	**3.2802**
Submit	**3446**	**199**	**3.2406**
Patient	**3568**	**77**	**3.1715**
Prideful	3524	121	2.8428
Grumble	3522	123	2.6633
Withhold judgment	3551	94	2.5736

Research Question Two. The second research question was, "What, if any, is the negative relationship between social media use and biblical interpersonal relationships as perceived by North American Christian college and seminary students?"

This question is examined by looking at each of the fifteen "one another sayings" Likert scale. An answer of negative was scored as a (1), somewhat negative was scored as a (2), no effect was scored as a (3), somewhat positive as a (4), and positive was scored as a Means below 3.00 indicate a positive overall perception of this characteristic of BIR. Three of the questions with a Likert scale had means that were less than 3.00 indicating that the subjects believed that social media was having a more negative effect on their BIR. These results are available in Table 36.

Table 36

Negative Perceptions

	Valid	Missing	M
Withhold judgment	**3551**	**94**	**2.5736**
Grumble	**3522**	**123**	**2.6633**
Prideful	**3524**	**121**	**2.8428**
Patient	3568	77	3.1715
Submit	3446	199	3.2406
Confess sins	3476	169	3.2802
Forgive	3511	134	3.3093
Peace	3555	90	3.3831
Warn	3520	125	3.5724
Hospitable	3538	107	3.8115
Love	3567	78	3.9151
Carry burdens	3557	88	3.9438
Kindness	3588	57	4.1265
Comfort	3574	71	4.2703
Encourage	3551	94	4.4734

Research Question Three. The third research question was, "What is the perceived effect of social media use on biblical interpersonal relationships among North American Christian college and seminary students?" To find this, the means of all fifteen Likert scale questions were considered together. The result was that the overall mean perception was 3.51. This showed that the perceived effect of social media use on BIR was positive. The respondents believed overall that social media is aiding them in their relationships with other Christians. For these results, see Table 37.

Table 37

Overall Perceptions

	Valid	Missing	*M*
Encourage	3551	94	4.4734
Comfort	3574	71	4.2703
Kindness	3588	57	4.1265
Carry burdens	3557	88	3.9438
Love	3567	78	3.9151
Hospitable	3538	107	3.8115
Warn	3520	125	3.5724
Peace	3555	90	3.3831
Forgive	3511	134	3.3093
Confess sins	3476	169	3.2802
Submit	3446	199	3.2406
Patient	3568	77	3.1715
Prideful	3524	121	2.8428
Grumble	3522	123	2.6633
Withhold judgment	3551	94	2.5736
Means Total	**3537**	**108**	**3.5052**

Results and the Sub-Problems

To further explore the results from the questionnaires, eight of the demographic categories were selected to explore. Each of the categories were compared with the fifteen characteristics of BIR.

Sub-Problem Research Question One. For the first sub-problem, *"What, if any, is the relationship between time spent in church activities and the perception of the effect of social media use on biblical interpersonal relationships among North American Christian college and seminary students?"* the mean difference of each category was compared.

When answering the question as to how many hours the respondent spend engaged in church activities, those who indicated they had spent twenty or more hours each week in church activities had a more positive response than other groups in seven of the characteristics of BIR. In the categories of *Withhold judgment* and *Grumble* the mean response of both groups were negative. Those who selected they spent between one and three hours in church activities had the more negative response. With the category of *Prideful*, there were mean responses both positive and negative. Those who spent four to seven hours in church activities had the most negative response, while those who were in church activities thirteen to twenty hours each week had the most positive response. Overall, those who spent eight or more hours at church each week had the most overall positive response with the highest mean falling within one of the categories that represented over eight hours engaged in church activities. These results are presented in Tables 38, 39, and 40.

Table 38

Summary: Hours spent in church activities

Church hours		Love	Encourage	Patient	Forgive	Comfort	Submit	Prideful
Less than 1	M	3.71	4.25	3.08	3.25	4.08	3.18	2.89
	N	562	562	570	563	570	542	560
	SD	1.02	0.87	1.05	0.96	0.91	0.85	0.96
1-3	M	3.93	4.49	3.16	3.33	4.29	3.24	2.80
	N	1417	1413	1412	1397	1422	1358	1408
	SD	0.94	0.72	1.08	0.92	0.81	0.85	1.00
4-7	M	3.94	4.51	3.17	3.27	4.30	3.25	**2.77**
	N	1005	995	1005	981	1000	979	989
	SD	0.92	0.68	1.02	0.91	0.78	0.86	0.99
8-12	M	4.04	4.58	3.27	**3.42**	4.35	3.29	3.01
	N	319	321	317	312	321	310	309
	SD	0.96	0.71	1.04	0.92	0.88	0.88	1.01
13-20	M	3.99	4.47	**3.37**	3.32	4.36	3.30	**3.09**
	N	92	91	92	90	91	88	89
	SD	0.98	0.79	1.06	0.96	0.86	0.91	0.98
More than 20	M	**4.09**	**4.60**	3.31	**3.42**	**4.41**	**3.34**	3.04
	N	172	169	172	168	170	169	169
	SD	0.82	0.59	1.07	0.93	0.69	0.82	0.93
Total	M	3.92	4.47	3.17	3.31	4.27	3.24	2.84
	N	3567	3551	3568	3511	3574	3446	3524
	SD	0.95	0.74	1.05	0.93	0.83	0.86	0.99

Table 39

Summary: Hours spent in church activities

Church Hours		Peace	Kindness	Judgment	Grumble	Hospitable	Confess sins	Carry burdens
Less than 1	M	3.32	3.96	2.55	2.62	3.73	3.21	3.63
	N	564	569	558	557	563	557	563
	SD	1.08	0.98	1.07	0.97	0.96	0.96	0.97
1-3	M	3.38	4.13	**2.54**	**2.61**	3.77	3.30	3.94
	N	1415	1428	1419	1400	1406	1366	1417
	SD	0.99	0.88	1.05	1.01	0.96	0.98	0.94
4-7	M	3.35	4.16	2.55	2.67	3.83	3.28	4.01
	N	1000	1004	999	999	998	991	998
	SD	1.02	0.85	1.04	1.04	0.92	0.99	0.88
8-12	M	**3.50**	**4.25**	2.73	2.84	3.95	**3.36**	4.13
	N	314	321	316	311	314	309	320
	SD	1.02	0.88	1.12	1.04	0.96	0.98	0.94
13-20	M	**3.50**	4.24	2.75	2.90	3.81	3.31	4.06
	N	90	92	92	92	86	91	90
	SD	0.96	0.88	1.12	0.98	1.01	1.01	0.95
More than 20	M	3.49	4.23	2.68	2.76	**3.98**	3.17	**4.25**
	N	172	174	167	163	171	162	169
	SD	1.03	0.86	1.01	1.02	0.92	1.03	0.79
Total	M	3.38	4.13	2.57	2.66	3.81	3.28	3.94
	N	3555	3588	3551	3522	3538	3476	3557
	SD	1.02	0.89	1.06	1.02	0.95	0.98	0.93

Table 40

Summary: Hours spent in church activities- Warn

Church hours	M	N	SD
Less than 1	3.4901	553	.97820
1-3	3.5360	1390	1.01241
4-7	3.5932	993	.98458
8-12	3.6426	319	1.02371
13-20	3.6304	92	1.12628
More than 20	**3.8497**	173	.94035
Total	3.5724	3520	1.00235

Sub-problem research question two. For the second sub-problem, *"What, if any, is the relationship between time spent using social media and the perception of the effect of social media use on biblical interpersonal relationships among North American Christian college and seminary students?"* the mean difference of each category was compared.

When answering the question as to how many hours the respondent spend engaged in social media, those who indicated they had spent twenty or more hours each week in social media activities had a more positive response than other groups in ten of the characteristics of BIR. In the categories of *Withhold judgment* and *Pride* the mean response of both groups were negative. Those who indicated they spent less than one hour in social media activities had the more negative response. In the category of *Grumble* the mean response of the group was negative. Those who indicated they spent between four and seven hours in social media activities had the more negative response. In the category of *Confess sins* the mean response of the group was positive. Those who indicated they spent between eight and twelve hours in social media activities had the more positive response. In the category of *Carry burdens* the mean response of the group was positive. Those who indicated they spent between one and three hours in social media activities had the more positive response.

Overall, those who spent eight or more hours in church activities each week had the most overall positive response with the highest mean falling within one of the categories that represented over eight hours engaged in social media. These results are presented in Tables 41, 42, and 43.

Table 41

Summary of social media hours

Social media hours		Love	Encourage	Patient	Forgive	Comfort	Submit	Pride
Less	M	3.49	4.05	2.95	2.98	3.91	3.07	**2.72**
than	N	186	187	185	183	186	185	181
1	SD	0.99	0.98	0.97	0.85	1.00	0.94	0.88
	M	3.89	4.43	3.10	3.25	4.23	3.23	2.84
1-3	N	761	755	757	745	758	737	749
	SD	0.91	0.75	1.03	0.89	0.81	0.83	0.99
	M	3.94	4.50	3.19	3.32	4.29	3.26	2.85
4-7	N	1133	1127	1127	1100	1134	1084	1118
	SD	0.93	0.70	1.04	0.90	0.81	0.81	0.97
	M	3.92	4.53	3.16	3.30	4.29	3.21	2.83
8-12	N	802	796	808	796	804	774	796
	SD	0.96	0.69	1.08	0.93	0.83	0.86	0.97
	M	3.94	4.51	3.20	3.36	4.30	3.16	2.82
13-20	N	378	379	381	381	383	367	374
	SD	0.95	0.72	1.07	0.93	0.81	0.83	1.01
More	M	**4.12**	**4.55**	**3.40**	**3.58**	**4.44**	**3.47**	2.98
than	N	295	295	298	296	297	288	294
20	SD	0.96	0.73	1.10	1.05	0.78	0.99	1.17
	M	3.91	4.47	3.17	3.31	4.27	3.24	2.84
Total	N	3555	3539	3556	3501	3562	3435	3512
	SD	0.95	0.74	1.05	0.93	0.83	0.86	0.99

Table 42

Summary of social media hours continued

Social media hours		Peace	Kindness	Judgment	Grumble	Hospitable	Confess sins	Carry Burdens
Less than 1	M	3.10	3.75	**2.47**	2.63	3.50	3.09	3.68
	N	186	188	184	184	185	184	186
	SD	.98	1.03	.90	.90	1.00	.96	1.09
1-3	M	3.35	4.04	2.61	2.72	3.72	3.20	3.94
	N	750	760	751	740	749	739	756
	SD	.99	.91	1.04	.98	.94	.92	.93
4-7	M	3.40	4.14	2.54	2.69	3.83	3.30	**3.99**
	N	1126	1138	1125	1114	1124	1102	1127
	SD	1.01	.88	1.01	1.03	.94	.93	.88
8-12	M	3.39	4.21	2.49	**2.55**	3.82	3.33	3.98
	N	802	809	806	798	795	786	799
	SD	1.02	.86	1.04	1.00	.94	1.00	.94
13-20	M	3.38	4.17	2.55	2.60	3.94	**3.34**	3.94
	N	381	382	379	381	381	367	383
	SD	1.00	.88	1.07	1.01	.92	.98	.95
More than 20	M	**3.56**	**4.26**	2.91	2.81	**3.95**	3.31	3.88
	N	298	299	294	295	292	287	294
	SD	1.08	.85	1.29	1.16	1.01	1.23	.98
Total	M	3.38	4.13	2.57	2.66	3.81	3.28	3.94
	N	3543	3576	3539	3512	3526	3465	3545
	SD	1.02	.89	1.06	1.02	.95	.98	.93

Table 43

Summary of social media hours continued: Warn

Social media hours	M	N	SD
Less than 1	3.3911	179	.97331
1-3	3.5340	751	.98447
4-7	3.5874	1115	.97280
8-12	3.5730	794	.99701
13-20	3.6111	378	1.04771
More than 20	**3.6826**	293	1.11571
Total	3.5732	3510	1.00252

Sub-problem research question three. For third sub-problem: *"What, if any, is the relationship between gender and the perception of the effect of social media use on biblical interpersonal relationships among North American Christian college and seminary students?"* the mean difference of each category was compared.

After examining all fifteen categories of BIR, it was discovered that in each response where the mean difference was significant ($p <$ .05), females either had a view that was more positive ($M > 3.00$) or more negative ($M < 3.00$) than males. The only exception with the question of the respondent's ability to warn other Christians about wrong behaviors. Three other categories did have responses with higher means for males than females, but those three categories were not found to have significantly different means ($p > .05$). These results are presented in Table 44.

Table 44

Summary

	Gender							
	Male			Female			Total	
	M	*N*	*SD*	*M*	*N*	*SD*	*p*	*MD*
Love	3.83	1626	.941	**3.98**	1941	.947	**.000**	.151
Encourage	4.38	1621	.789	**4.54**	1930	.681	**.000**	.163
Patient	**3.18**	1616	1.038	3.15	1952	1.066	.391	.030
Forgive	**3.31**	1591	.907	3.30	1920	.939	.717	.011
Comfort	4.19	1624	.842	**4.33**	1950	.810	**.000**	.137
Submit	3.22	1592	.867	**3.25**	1854	.844	.282	.031
Prideful	2.90	1602	.968	**2.79**	1922	1.009	**.002**	.106
Peace	**3.39**	1615	1.002	3.37	1940	1.027	.480	.024
Kindness	4.02	1632	.918	**4.20**	1956	.861	**.000**	.179
Judgment	2.65	1615	1.029	**2.50**	1936	1.072	**.000**	.143
Grumble	2.73	1595	1.022	**2.60**	1927	1.011	**.000**	.128
Hospitable	3.76	1604	.939	**3.84**	1934	.959	**.013**	.079
Confess sins	3.25	1593	.988	**3.30**	1883	.974	.173	.045
Carry burdens	3.90	1614	.936	**3.97**	1943	.930	**.011**	.079
Warn	**3.61**	1613	1.017	3.54	1907	.988	**.041**	.069
Means	3.49	1610	.947	3.51	1926	.941		

Note. *M* = 3.00 indicates *No Effect*. For each mean comparison the higher mean is emboldened if the number is over 3.00 to indicate the most positive response. If the number is below 3.00 then the lower of the two means is emboldened to indicate the most negative response.

Sub-problem research question four. For third sub-problem: *"What, if any, is the relationship between age and the perception of the effect of social media use on biblical interpersonal relationships among North American Christian college and seminary students?"* the mean difference of each category was compared.

When answering the question as to their age category, the most positive mean responses were distributed across four of the seven categories. First, those who indicated they were seventeen and younger had a more positive response than other groups in five of the characteristics of BIR—*Hospitable, Confess sins, Warn, Comfort,* and *Submit.* Next, those who indicated they were forty to forty-nine had a more positive response than other groups in two of the characteristics of BIR—*Love* and *Kindness.* Next, those who indicated they were fifty to fifty-nine had a more positive response than other groups in three of the characteristics of BIR—*Prideful, Carry burdens,* and *Peace.* Finally, those who indicated they were sixty and older had a more positive response than other groups in the final four characteristics of BIR—*Patient, Forgive, Judgment,* and *Grumble.* Overall, those who were forty and over had a more positive response than those who were younger. The exception being the less than one percent of respondents who were seventeen and younger. These results are presented in Tables 45 and 46.

Table 45

Summary of Age Categories

Age		Love	Patient	Forgive	Comfort	Submit	Prideful	Peace
17 or younger	M	4.04	3.50	3.50	**4.50**	**3.50**	2.95	3.83
	N	24	24	24	24	22	23	24
	SD	1.04	.88	.97	.65	.85	.97	1.04
18-20	M	3.91	3.15	3.25	4.24	3.20	2.81	3.32
	N	1169	1174	1160	1170	1141	1164	1170
	SD	.95	1.05	.92	.84	.84	.98	1.00
21-29	M	3.87	3.06	3.26	4.25	3.19	2.73	3.32
	N	1545	1549	1521	1555	1491	1536	1544
	SD	.95	1.04	.92	.82	.84	.98	1.02
30-39	M	3.83	3.12	3.34	4.27	3.24	2.89	3.34
	N	404	403	399	403	394	399	401
	SD	.91	1.05	.84	.82	.84	.97	.98
40-49	M	**4.18**	3.59	3.58	4.41	3.48	3.27	3.76
	N	222	217	215	218	204	211	217
	SD	.87	1.05	.93	.75	.92	1.00	.98
50-59	M	4.08	3.65	3.53	4.44	3.48	**3.29**	**3.86**
	N	159	157	150	158	153	152	155
	SD	.85	.91	.99	.70	.85	.86	.91
60 or older	M	4.02	**3.68**	**3.73**	4.17	3.39	3.28	3.68
	N	44	44	42	46	41	39	44
	SD	.97	.95	.82	1.03	.91	.94	.93
Total	M	3.91	3.17	3.30	4.27	3.24	2.84	3.38
	N	3567	3568	3511	3574	3446	3524	3555
	SD	.94	1.05	.92	.82	.85	.99	1.01

Table 46

Summary of Age Categories

Age		Kindness	Judgment	Grumble	Hospitable	Confess sins	Carry burdens	Warn
17 or younger	M	4.20	2.41	2.82	**4.12**	**3.86**	4.08	**3.95**
	N	24	24	23	24	23	24	24
	SD	.97	.97	.98	1.03	.69	.88	.90
18-20	M	4.11	2.45	2.57	3.78	3.32	3.84	3.57
	N	1173	1169	1163	1159	1157	1169	1167
	SD	.89	1.01	.99	.92	.97	.94	.99
21-29	M	4.10	2.47	2.55	3.76	3.26	3.90	3.53
	N	1557	1546	1537	1535	1506	1541	1515
	SD	.89	1.05	.98	.96	.98	.93	1.02
30-39	M	4.09	2.65	2.81	3.80	3.20	4.00	3.58
	N	407	398	401	399	393	403	399
	SD	.88	.98	1.00	.91	.90	.93	.97
40-49	M	**4.30**	3.19	3.16	4.03	3.29	4.30	3.66
	N	223	215	212	220	210	218	219
	SD	.86	1.04	1.04	.93	1.07	.78	.98
50-59	M	4.29	3.17	3.21	4.10	3.29	**4.30**	3.76
	N	159	156	147	157	147	156	153
	SD	.81	1.03	1.09	.93	1.00	.78	.84
60 or older	M	4.06	**3.44**	**3.28**	3.93	2.90	4.04	3.27
	N	45	43	39	44	40	46	43
	SD	1.13	1.05	.99	1.02	.87	1.01	1.07
Total	M	4.12	2.57	2.66	3.81	3.28	3.94	3.57
	N	3588	3551	3522	3538	3476	3557	3520
	SD	.89	1.05	1.01	.95	.98	.93	1.00

Sub-problem research question five. For the fifth sub-problem: *"What, if any, is the relationship between the whether or not a subject has shared his/her faith through social media and the perception of the effect of social media use on biblical interpersonal relationships among North American Christian college and seminary students?"* the mean difference of each category was compared.

When answering the question as to whether or not a subject had used a social media platform to share their faith with another person, those who indicated they had prayed with another person had a more positive response than those who had not in thirteen of the characteristics of BIR. In the categories of *Prideful, Withhold judgment,* and *Grumble* the mean response of both groups were negative. Those who selected they had not shared their faith with another person had a more negative response than those who had. These results are presented in Table 47.

Table 47

Summary: Have you ever shared your faith through social media?

	Yes			No			Total		
	M	*N*	*SD*	*M*	*N*	*SD*	*M*	*N*	*SD*
Love	**3.98**	2960	.93	3.55	607	.92	3.91	3567	.94
Encourage	**4.54**	2944	.68	4.14	607	.87	4.47	3551	.73
Patient	**3.21**	2966	1.07	2.95	602	.93	3.17	3568	1.05
Forgive	**3.35**	2921	.94	3.10	590	.81	3.30	3511	.92
Comfort	**4.33**	2962	.79	3.95	612	.92	4.27	3574	.82
Submit	**3.28**	2858	.87	3.04	588	.73	3.24	3446	.85
Prideful	2.86	2928	1.00	**2.74**	596	.90	2.84	3524	.99
Peace	**3.42**	2957	1.02	3.17	598	.94	3.38	3555	1.01
Kindness	**4.18**	2976	.86	3.83	612	.94	4.12	3588	.89
Judgment	2.59	2946	1.07	**2.48**	605	.95	2.57	3551	1.05
Grumble	2.67	2923	1.04	**2.60**	599	.89	2.66	3522	1.01
Hospitable	**3.87**	2935	.94	3.50	603	.91	3.81	3538	.95
Confess sins	**3.32**	2893	.99	3.06	583	.85	3.28	3476	.98
Carry burdens	**3.99**	2951	.93	3.68	606	.90	3.94	3557	.93
Warn	**3.63**	2926	1.00	3.26	594	.92	3.57	3520	1.00
Means	3.55	2936	.94	3.27	600	.89	3.50	3537	.94

Sub-problem research question six. For the sixth sub-problem, *"What, if any, is the relationship between the whether or not a subject has prayed with someone through social media and the perception of the effect of social media use on biblical interpersonal relationships among North American Christian college and seminary students?"* the mean difference of each category was compared.

When answering the question as to whether or not a subject had used a social media platform to pray with another person, those who indicated they had prayed with another person had a more positive response than those who had not in fourteen of the characteristics of BIR. In the category of *Withhold judgment,* the mean response of both groups were negative. Those who selected they had not prayed with another person had a more negative response than those who had. Also, with the category of *Grumble,* the mean response of both groups were the same ($M = 2.66$). These results are presented in Table 48.

Table 48

Summary: Have you ever prayed with someone through social media?

	Yes			No			Total		
	Mean	*N*	*SD*	*M*	*N*	*SD*	*M*	*N*	*SD*
Love	**4.02**	2159	.92	3.74	1392	.95	3.91	3551	.94
Encourage	**4.59**	2153	.63	4.28	1382	.83	4.47	3535	.73
Patient	**3.22**	2165	1.09	3.09	1387	.98	3.17	3552	1.05
Forgive	**3.37**	2134	.95	3.19	1361	.86	3.30	3495	.92
Comfort	**4.38**	2161	.77	4.09	1397	.87	4.27	3558	.82
Submit	**3.30**	2085	.89	3.14	1346	.77	3.24	3431	.85
Prideful	**2.85**	2136	1.01	2.81	1372	.94	2.84	3508	.99
Peace	**3.48**	2160	1.03	3.22	1381	.96	3.38	3541	1.01
Kindness	**4.21**	2171	.86	3.98	1401	.91	4.12	3572	.89
Judgment	**2.61**	2152	1.09	2.51	1383	.99	2.57	3535	1.05
Grumble	**2.66**	2138	1.04	**2.66**	1368	.98	2.66	3506	1.01
Hospitable	**3.89**	2147	.94	3.68	1376	.94	3.81	3523	.95
Confess sins	**3.38**	2106	1.01	3.12	1354	.90	3.27	3460	.98
Carry burdens	**4.05**	2158	.91	3.76	1383	.93	3.94	3541	.93
Warn	**3.63**	2137	1.01	3.47	1368	.96	3.57	3505	1.00
Means	3.58	2144	.94	3.38	1376	.92	3.50	3520	.94

Sub-problem research question seven. *"What, if any, is the relationship between the what format a student takes his/her coursework and the perception of the effect of social media use on biblical interpersonal relationships among North American Christian college and seminary students?"* the mean difference of each category was compared.

When answering the question as to what in what format a subject takes classes, those who indicated they were distances learning students had a more positive response than those who took classes on campus in twelve categories. In the categories of *Withhold judgment and Grumble,* the mean response of both groups were negative and those on campus had the most negative view. Only in the category of *Confess sins* was did on campus students have both a positive view and a higher mean response than those who were online. These results are presented in Table 48.

Table 48

Summary Report: In what format do you take classes?

	On Campus			Online/Distance Learning			Total		
	M	*N*	*SD*	*M*	*N*	*SD*	*M*	*N*	*SD*
Love	3.89	3118	.95	**4.02**	449	.88	3.91	3567	.94
Encourage	4.46	3098	.74	**4.54**	453	.65	4.47	3551	.73
Patient	3.15	3120	1.05	**3.31**	448	1.03	3.17	3568	1.05
Forgive	3.28	3068	.92	**3.46**	443	.90	3.30	3511	.92
Comfort	4.25	3124	.84	**4.40**	450	.72	4.27	3574	.82
Submit	3.21	3013	.85	**3.39**	433	.83	3.24	3446	.85
Prideful	2.81	3085	.98	**3.02**	439	.99	2.84	3524	.99
Peace	3.35	3108	1.01	**3.59**	447	.99	3.38	3555	1.01
Kindness	4.11	3132	.90	**4.21**	456	.82	4.12	3588	.89
Judgment	**2.55**	3102	1.06	2.73	449	.99	2.57	3551	1.05
Grumble	**2.62**	3085	1.01	2.89	437	.99	2.66	3522	1.01
Hospitable	3.79	3094	.96	**3.89**	444	.87	3.81	3538	.95
Confess sins	**3.28**	3043	.97	3.23	433	.99	3.28	3476	.98
Carry burdens	3.90	3110	.94	**4.18**	447	.81	3.94	3557	.93
Warn	3.55	3075	1.00	**3.71**	445	.93	3.57	3520	1.00
Means	3.48	3092	.95	**3.64**	445	.89	3.50	3537	.94

Sub-problem research question eight. For the eight sub-problem, *"What, if any, is the relationship between class rank and the perception of the effect of social media use on biblical interpersonal relationships among North American Christian college and seminary students?"* the mean difference of each category was compared.

When answering the question as to their class rank, those who indicated they were doctoral students had a more positive response than other groups in seven of the characteristics of BIR. In the category *Prideful,* doctoral students were the only group to have a positive mean ($M = 3.04$). Freshmen had the more positive responses in four categories—*Confess sins, Encourage, Warn,* and *Patient.* In the categories of *Withhold judgment* and *Grumble* the mean response of both groups were negative. Those who indicated they were seniors had the more negative response in both categories. Graduate students had the most positive perception in the category of *Comfort.* Overall, doctoral students had the highest mean perception of social media effect on BIR ($M = 3.61$). Freshmen were second most positive and graduate students were third. These results are presented in Tables 49 and 50.

Table 49

Summary: Class Rank

Class Rank:		Encourage		Forgive		Submit	
	Love		Patient		Comfort		Prideful
Fr.	M 3.982	**4.529**	**3.303**	3.383	4.327	3.255	2.944
	N 561	560	564	551	562	545	551
	SD .975	.734	1.067	.952	.831	.874	.994
So.	M 3.926	4.449	3.298	3.319	4.258	3.313	2.889
	N 591	584	591	587	592	579	588
	SD .939	.773	1.048	.943	.836	.889	1.023
Jr.	M 3.899	4.452	3.062	3.240	4.219	3.216	2.748
	N 624	626	626	621	635	602	623
	SD .954	.734	1.080	.933	.858	.836	.995
Sr.	M 3.835	4.404	3.009	3.228	4.177	3.126	2.721
	N 653	651	653	645	651	620	646
	SD .958	.761	1.067	.934	.842	.822	.951
Grad	M 3.924	4.519	3.182	3.346	**4.335**	3.262	2.868
	N 972	967	970	943	970	942	960
	SD .931	.696	1.008	.880	.780	.850	.995
Doc	M **3.976**	4.460	3.262	**3.402**	4.305	**3.342**	**3.038**
	N 166	163	164	164	164	158	156
	SD .901	.747	1.032	.932	.839	.865	.929
Total	M 3.915	4.473	3.172	3.309	4.270	3.241	2.843
	N 3567	3551	3568	3511	3574	3446	3524
	SD .947	.737	1.054	.925	.828	.856	.992

Table 50

Summary: Class Rank continued

Class Rank:		Peace	Kind	WH	Grum.	Hos.	Conf.	Car.	Warn
	M	3.44	4.17	2.63	2.71	3.86	**3.40**	3.91	3.73
Fr.	N	554	564	553	554	556	547	552	557
	SD	1.03	0.88	1.07	1.02	0.91	0.98	0.96	0.98
	M	3.42	4.13	2.54	2.68	3.83	3.39	3.90	3.62
So.	N	595	592	594	585	592	582	597	589
	SD	1.00	0.91	1.05	1.01	0.93	0.93	0.96	0.98
	M	3.32	4.11	2.46	2.58	3.77	3.26	3.83	3.46
Jr.	N	631	631	630	623	619	614	630	620
	SD	1.03	0.88	1.08	1.03	0.98	1.02	0.92	1.03
	M	3.30	4.07	**2.44**	**2.52**	3.74	3.26	3.88	3.44
Sr.	N	649	657	649	647	646	627	650	634
	SD	1.03	0.93	1.01	0.99	0.97	0.93	0.91	1.01
	M	3.40	4.13	2.67	2.75	3.83	3.21	4.06	3.60
Grad	N	963	979	963	957	961	946	963	955
	SD	1.01	0.87	1.05	1.02	0.95	1.00	0.93	0.99
	M	**3.57**	**4.22**	2.89	2.87	**3.93**	3.04	**4.22**	3.66
Doc	N	163	165	162	156	164	160	165	165
	SD	0.97	0.88	1.02	1.09	0.94	0.98	0.78	0.93
	M	3.38	4.13	2.57	2.66	3.81	3.28	3.94	3.57
Total	N	3555	3588	3551	3522	3538	3476	3557	3520
	SD	1.02	0.89	1.06	1.02	0.95	0.98	0.93	1.00

5 CONCLUSIONS

After the analysis of the data that was collected during this study, it was possible to draw numerous conclusions about the perceptions of NACCSS about social media's effect on their relationships. As will be discussed below, many of these conclusions did not align with what the researcher hypothesized. After reexamining the research purpose and questions, this chapter will explore some concluding thoughts on this study.

Research Implications

There are several implications that arise from the results of this study. First, the researcher found it interesting that though online/distance learning students spent more time in church (M = 3.29) and less time using social media (M = 3.13), they had a more positive perception of social media's effect on BIR in twelve of the categories and an overall higher perception (M = 3.64) than on campus students. This is due, in part, to the fact that the mean age of students who are online are older (On Campus = 2. 94;

Online/Distance Learning = 4.18).

Adding to this are the results that seem to refute a colloquial belief that older people have antipathy toward and are not using social media. At least among this subsection of that population, social media is being consumed and consumed often. It should not be ignored that, in every age category, the mean response was above the four to seven hours per week in social media category. That is over an hour per day.

This study also mirrored several of the questions from Auday and Colman (2009) and was insightful to see changes that had taken place in the three years since their study. Their study primarily questioned those who were 18-27 years old. Their results were compared with those in this current study who indicated they were in the *17 and younger*, *18-21*, and the *22-29* categories. They reported that 93% of their respondents had Facebook accounts and this current study echoed that with 95% of respondents indicated they had some type social media account (p. 3). In contrast, when asked about the time spent using social media, the results were contrary to the findings of Auday and Coleman.

They estimated students were spending about 18.6 hours each week in social networking activities (p. 3). The mean time spent in social media of the respondents in this current was between the categories of *4-7* and *8-12* hours each week (M = 3.46). In part, this difference may be due to the way the question was answered. Auday and Coleman asked for a daily estimate whereas this current study asked for weekly estimates. The previous study also found that the respondents did not believe that social media was causing their relationships to suffer. Both studies revealed that they had an overall perception that was more positive. However this study (M = 3.46) had a higher over positive perception that then previous study (M = 3.07). This may reveal a trend toward a more positive perception of social media.

Research Applications

This researcher believes that there are many applications that come out as a result of this study. The study, in the end, covered a wide range of questions, many of which need to be carefully nuanced. They have relevance for both Christian higher education and the Church.

First, for higher education, it is clear that social media cannot be ignored. Students in the typical college age category, 18-22, are going to church less and using social media more. These students believe that social media, overall, is having a positive effect on their relationships. They are using this communication medium to both share their faith and pray with other people. This study did not assess the success of these endeavors, but it was surprising to find that this phenomenon was occurring. Those students who are praying with others and sharing their faith have a much more positive view. This leads the researcher to believe that these students, at least in part, are using social media for edifying activities. Schools, therefore, should consider how they will harness the power of social media to build relationships within the student body.

Secondly for schools, it should be observed that older students are also using social media and find it having a positive effect on their relationships. These are students that are active in their church and are also using social media to share their faith. In fact, there was no significant difference between those over forty and those under forty when it came to whether or not they had shared through social media ($p > .05$). With this observation, schools should not be hesitant to use social media with their non-traditional students. Obviously, this social media use trend might not be applicable to the older age categories at-large. However, institutes of higher education are not working with the general population of older students, but those who have either come to school or back to school to further their education. These students have indicated that they are using social media.

For the church, the implications are not entirely different. The youngest categories surveyed are attending church much less than those who are older. This trend may be somewhat misleading as many of those in older categories may be employed by churches as they were more typically seminary students. Nevertheless, these students do not seem to be as engaged in church activities as they could be. The question churches must ask is how they can use social media to encourage students toward church activities. Christian students seem willing to use social media for spiritual activities, affording churches the ability to use this social media to engage their students, build community, and encourage students toward fellowship with others.

Future Research

The research from this study revealed that NACCSS believe that social media is having an overall positive effect on their relationships ($M = 3.51$). Unfortunately, the nature of this study does not allow the researcher to answer some of the most pressing "why" questions from that have arisen. For example, why do those who are older give such high marks to social media when they are spending less time engaged in it? These questions show the need for qualitative research that can answer these questions. A smaller group of these students need to be personally interviewed and their perception expanded upon.

It would also be prudent to consider how students are actually using social media. This could be done in a two-fold manner. First, students should be surveyed for their disclosure of their activities in social media. They can be asked what they post to websites, what for what purpose they typically use mediums like email, and about things that others communicate to them online. After this is done, those same student's social media accounts would be examined and coded to determine if their perceptions of what is happening online is really what is occurring. These same characteristics of BIR could be used to code their activities online.

Because those who spent the most time in church activities had the overall highest positive perception of social media's effect on the BIR, it may be important to find out how participants in that category are using social media. In ten out of fifteen categories, those who were forty or over had the highest mean positive views. They also spent significantly more time in church ($p < .05$) than those under forty. This was not expected and therefore could be explored in the future for valuable information about

Final Summary

Carr (2010) asks the question, "What is the Internet doing to our brains?" In exploring the answer to the question he looks at the life and writings of Joseph Weizenbaum (1976). Weizenbaum created a computer program more than four decades ago, called ELIZA. This program allowed humans to "talk" to computers and the computer would respond back to what information was entered by the user. This program caught on quickly became vogue throughout the country, especially on college campuses. Different researchers soon began to see the promise for this new technology in fields beyond the realm of novelty. Weizenbaum, however, began to be concerned about his own creation. Carr encapsulates Weizenbaum's writings:

> What makes us most human, Weizenbaum had come to believe, is what is least computable about us—the connections between our mind and our body, the experiences that shape our memory and our thinking, our capacity for emotion and empathy. The great danger we face as we become more intimately involved with our computers—as we come to experience more of our lives through the

disembodied symbols flickering across our screens—is that we'll begin to lose our humanness, to sacrifice the very qualities that separate us from machines. The only way to avoid that fate, Weizenbaum wrote, is to have the self-awareness and the courage to refuse to delegate to computers the most human of our mental activities and intellectual pursuits, particularly 'tasks that demand wisdom.' (pp.207-208)

Weizenbaum writing in the 1970s and Clark in a contemporary context saw the reality of trading human activities for computerized interaction. The overall research is mixed but few doubt that the impact is substantial.

The results from this study revealed that NACCSS believe that social media is having an overall positive effect on their BIR. Students are using this communication tool to share their faith and pray with others. With the exponential growth of this means of communication and the growing use across all demographics, it is of vital importance for believers to remember that the calling of Christ is a calling into a community. The respondents in this study believe that social media is helping them to build this community by having a positive effect on their relationships. Since students believe that social media can have this effect, church leaders and higher education administrators should encourage those who they mentor to ensure that social media is being used for edification. The exhortation of those who are in positions of the authority should be that of the writer of the Letter to the Hebrews as they work with students who are walking through life with social media in hand:

Therefore, brothers, since we have confidence to enter the holy places by the blood of Jesus, by the new and living way that he opened for us through the curtain,

that is, through his flesh, and since we have a great priest over the house of God, let us draw near with a true heart in full assurance of faith, with our hearts sprinkled clean from an evil conscience and our bodies washed with pure water. Let us hold fast the confession of our hope without wavering, for he who promised is faithful. And let us consider how to stir up one another to love and good works, not neglecting to meet together, as is the habit of some, but encouraging one another, and all the more as you see the **Day drawing near.** (Heb 10:19-25 ESV)

6 APPENDICIES

Social Media Questionnaire

Thank you for participating in this survey. We want you to think about how your use of social media (the Internet, Facebook, Twitter, cell phone, etc.) effects your relationships with other Christians. Please read each question carefully and consider how social media effects different aspects of your relationships with other Christians. No personal information from this survey will be shared with your school or anyone outside the research team. By submitting this questionnaire, you are consenting for your answers to be used to compile data for a dissertation being written by Micheal Pardue, a doctoral student at Southeastern Baptist Theological Seminary. The data may also be used for future research done by the One Another Project. The results of this study will be made available at www.oneanotherproject.org once the study is complete. If you have questions or concerns about this questionnaire, please call (###) ###-#### or email info@oneanotherproject.org.

Everyone who participates in this survey will be entered in a drawing to win one of four $25 dollar gift cards to Amazon.com. After we have finished data collection, we will conduct the drawing. Winners will receive notification of the gift card via e-mail.

Name: _____

Do you consider yourself a Christian?

1. Yes
2. No

Gender:
1. Male
2. Female

School: _____

In what format do you take classes?

1. On Campus
2. Online/Distance Learning

Class Rank:

1. Freshman
2. Sophomore
3. Junior
4. Senior
5. Graduate Student

Age:

1. 17 or younger
2. 18-20
3. 21-29
4. 30-39
5. 40-49

6. 50-59
7. 60 or older

About how many hours a week do you spend using social media?

1. Less than 1
2. 1-3
3. 4-7
4. 8-12
5. 13-20
6. More than 20

About how many hours a week do you spend in activities organized by your local church?

1. Less than 1
2. 1-3
3. 4-7
4. 8-12
5. 13-20
6. More than 20

Please check which of these you own:

1. PC
2. Mac
3. Tablet
4. Smart phone

Please check which social media you use:

1. Networking sites on your computer or tablet (Facebook, Twitter, LinkedIn, Myspace, etc.)
2. Networking sites on your smart phone (Facebook, Twitter, LinkedIn, Myspace, etc.)
3. Video sharing sites (YouTube, Vimeo, etc.)
4. Email
5. Text messaging
6. Cell phone calls
7. The Internet

Have you ever shared your faith through social media?

1. Yes
2. No

Have you ever prayed with someone through social media?

1. Yes
2. No

1. What effect does social media have on your ability to love other Christians?

Negative	Somewhat Negative	No Effect	Somewhat Positive	Positive
1.	2.	3.	4.	5.

2. What effect does social media have on your ability to encourage other Christians?

Negative	Somewhat Negative	No Effect	Somewhat Positive	Positive
1.	2.	3.	4.	5.

3. What effect does social media have on your ability to be patient with other Christians?

Negative	Somewhat Negative	No Effect	Somewhat Positive	Positive
1.	2.	3.	4.	5.

4. What effect does social media have on your ability to forgive other Christians?

Negative	Somewhat Negative	No Effect	Somewhat Positive	Positive
1.	2.	3.	4.	5.

5. What effect does social media have on your ability to comfort other Christians?

Negative	Somewhat Negative	No Effect	Somewhat Positive	Positive
1.	2.	3.	4.	5.

6. What effect does social media have on your ability to submit to other Christians?

Negative	Somewhat Negative	No Effect	Somewhat Positive	Positive
1.	2.	3.	4.	5.

7. What effect does social media have on your ability not to be prideful toward other Christians?

Negative	Somewhat Negative	No Effect	Somewhat Positive	Positive
1.	2.	3.	4.	5.

8. What effect does social media have on your ability to be at peace with other Christians?

Negative	Somewhat Negative	No Effect	Somewhat Positive	Positive
1.	2.	3.	4.	5.

9. What effect does social media have on your ability to show kindness to other Christians?

Negative	Somewhat Negative	No Effect	Somewhat Positive	Positive
1.	2.	3.	4.	5.

10. What effect does social media have on your ability to withhold judgment from other Christians?

Negative	Somewhat Negative	No Effect	Somewhat Positive	Positive
1.	2.	3.	4.	5.

11. What effect does social media have on your ability not to grumble against other Christians?

Negative   Somewhat Negative   No Effect   Somewhat Positive   Positive
1.   2.   3.   4.   5.

12. What effect does social media have on your ability to be hospitable to other Christians?

Negative   Somewhat Negative   No Effect   Somewhat Positive   Positive
1.   2.   3.   4.   5.

13. What effect does social media have on your ability to confess your sins to other Christians?

Negative   Somewhat Negative   No Effect   Somewhat Positive   Positive
1.   2.   3.   4.   5.

14. What effect does social media have on your ability to carry the burdens of other Christians?

Negative   Somewhat Negative   No Effect   Somewhat Positive   Positive
1.   2.   3.   4.   5.

15. What effect does social media have on your ability to warn other Christians about their wrong behaviors?

Negative   Somewhat Negative   No Effect   Somewhat Positive   Positive
1.   2.   3.   4.   5.

16. Do you have an account on a social networking website (like Facebook or Myspace)?
1. Yes
2. No

17. About how many of your "friends" on Facebook have you met in person?

1. All of them
2. Most of them
3. About half of them
4. A few of them
5. None of them

Summary Tables and Figures

Table 51

Love

Demographic Categories	Variable	M
Gender	Male	3.8327
	Female	3.9840
Class Delivery:	On Campus	3.8993
	Online/Distance Learning	4.0245
Age:	17 or younger	4.0417
	18-20	3.9136
	21-29	3.8738
	30-39	3.8391
	40-49	4.1892
	50-59	4.0881
	60 or older	4.0227
Class Rank:	Freshman	3.9822
	Sophomore	3.9255
	Junior	3.8990
	Senior	3.8346
	Graduate Student	3.9239
	Doctoral Student	3.9759
Church Activity Hours:	Less than 1	3.7135
	1-3	3.9252
	4-7	3.9353
	8-12	4.0439
	13-20	3.9891
	More than 20	4.0930
Social Media Hours:	Less than 1	3.4892
	1-3	3.8870
	4-7	3.9356
	8-12	3.9190
	13-20	3.9418
	More than 20	4.1186
Prayed?	Yes	3.9895
	No	3.5519
Shared Faith?	Yes	4.0269
	No	3.7435
Total		**3.9151**

Table 52

Encourage

Demographic Categories	Variable	M
Gender	Male	4.3843
	Female	4.5482
Class Delivery:	On Campus	4.4626
	Online/Distance Learning	4.5475
Age:	17 or younger	4.6667
	18-20	4.4599
	21-29	4.4581
	30-39	4.4788
	40-49	4.5955
	50-59	4.5570
	60 or older	4.3043
Class Rank:	Freshman	4.5286
	Sophomore	4.4486
	Junior	4.4521
	Senior	4.4040
	Graduate Student	4.5191
	Doctoral Student	4.4601
Church Activity Hours:	Less than 1	4.2527
	1-3	4.4940
	4-7	4.5136
	8-12	4.5763
	13-20	4.4725
	More than 20	4.6036
Social Media Hours:	Less than 1	4.0535
	1-3	4.4252
	4-7	4.5022
	8-12	4.5327
	13-20	4.5145
	More than 20	4.5492
Prayed?	Yes	4.5941
	No	4.2873
Shared Faith?	Yes	4.5421
	No	4.1400
Total		**4.4734**

Table 53
Patient

Demographic Categories	Variable	M
Gender	Male	3.1881
	Female	3.1578
Class Delivery:	On Campus	3.1513
	Online/Distance Learning	3.3125
Age:	17 or younger	3.5000
	18-20	3.1550
	21-29	3.0671
	30-39	3.1290
	40-49	3.5945
	50-59	3.6561
	60 or older	3.6818
Class Rank:	Freshman	3.2978
	Sophomore	3.0623
	Junior	3.0092
	Senior	3.1825
	Graduate Student	3.2622
	Doctoral Student	3.3032
Church Activity Hours:	Less than 1	3.0807
	1-3	3.1579
	4-7	3.1692
	8-12	3.2713
	13-20	3.3696
	More than 20	3.3081
Social Media Hours:	Less than 1	2.9459
	1-3	3.1030
	4-7	3.1890
	8-12	3.1559
	13-20	3.2047
	More than 20	3.3993
Prayed?	Yes	3.2208
	No	3.0923
Shared Faith?	Yes	3.2165
	No	2.9502
Total		**3.1715**

Table 54
Forgive

Demographic Categories	Variable	M
Gender	Male	3.3155
	Female	3.3042
Class Delivery:	On Campus	3.2868
	Online/Distance Learning	3.4650
Age:	17 or younger	3.5000
	18-20	3.2569
	21-29	3.2630
	30-39	3.3484
	40-49	3.5860
	50-59	3.5333
	60 or older	3.7381
Class Rank:	Freshman	3.3186
	Sophomore	3.2399
	Junior	3.2279
	Senior	3.3457
	Graduate Student	3.4024
	Doctoral Student	3.3829
Church Activity Hours:	Less than 1	3.2451
	1-3	3.3278
	4-7	3.2650
	8-12	3.4167
	13-20	3.3222
	More than 20	3.4226
Social Media Hours:	Less than 1	2.9836
	1-3	3.2510
	4-7	3.3200
	8-12	3.2965
	13-20	3.3570
	More than 20	3.5777
Prayed?	Yes	3.3786
	No	3.1991
Shared Faith?	Yes	3.3506
	No	3.1051
Total		**3.3093**

Table 55
Comfort

Demographic Categories	Variable	M
Gender	Male	4.1952
	Female	4.3328
Class Delivery:	On Campus	4.2503
	Online/Distance Learning	4.4089
Age:	17 or younger	4.5000
	18-20	4.2436
	21-29	4.2508
	30-39	4.2730
	40-49	4.4174
	50-59	4.4430
	60 or older	4.1739
Class Rank:	Freshman	4.2584
	Sophomore	4.2189
	Junior	4.1767
	Senior	4.3351
	Graduate Student	4.3049
	Doctoral Student	4.3274
Church Activity Hours:	Less than 1	4.0842
	1-3	4.2876
	4-7	4.2960
	8-12	4.3458
	13-20	4.3626
	More than 20	4.4059
Social Media Hours:	Less than 1	3.9140
	1-3	4.2348
	4-7	4.2857
	8-12	4.2873
	13-20	4.3003
	More than 20	4.4377
Prayed?	Yes	4.3359
	No	3.9526
Shared Faith?	Yes	4.3818
	No	4.0981
Total		**4.2704**

Table 56
Submit

Demographic Categories	Variable	M
Gender	Male	3.2236
	Female	3.2551
Class Delivery:	On Campus	3.2187
	Online/Distance Learning	3.3926
Age:	17 or younger	3.5000
	18-20	3.2086
	21-29	3.1979
	30-39	3.2462
	40-49	3.4804
	50-59	3.4837
	60 or older	3.3902
Class Rank:	Freshman	3.3126
	Sophomore	3.2159
	Junior	3.1258
	Senior	3.2622
	Graduate Student	3.3418
	Doctoral Student	3.2550
Church Activity Hours:	Less than 1	3.1771
	1-3	3.2356
	4-7	3.2451
	8-12	3.2903
	13-20	3.2955
	More than 20	3.3373
Social Media Hours:	Less than 1	3.0703
	1-3	3.2347
	4-7	3.2611
	8-12	3.2132
	13-20	3.1553
	More than 20	3.4688
Prayed?	Yes	3.3046
	No	3.1434
Shared Faith?	Yes	3.2806
	No	3.0459
Total		**3.2406**

Table 57
Prideful

Demographic Categories	Variable	M
Gender	Male	2.9007
	Female	2.7945
Class Delivery:	On Campus	2.8172
	Online/Distance Learning	3.0228
Age:	17 or younger	2.9565
	18-20	2.8101
	21-29	2.7357
	30-39	2.8997
	40-49	3.2749
	50-59	3.2961
	60 or older	3.2821
Class Rank:	Freshman	2.8895
	Sophomore	2.7480
	Junior	2.7214
	Senior	2.8677
	Graduate Student	3.0385
	Doctoral Student	2.9437
Church Activity Hours:	Less than 1	2.8857
	1-3	2.8004
	4-7	2.7725
	8-12	3.0065
	13-20	3.0899
	More than 20	3.0355
Social Media Hours:	Less than 1	2.7182
	1-3	2.8411
	4-7	2.8524
	8-12	2.8254
	13-20	2.8182
	More than 20	2.9830
Prayed?	Yes	2.8586
	No	2.8141
Shared Faith?	Yes	2.8634
	No	2.7416
Total		**2.8428**

Table 58
Peace

Demographic Categories	Variable	M
Gender	Male	3.3963
	Female	3.3722
Class Delivery:	On Campus	3.3530
	Online/Distance Learning	3.5928
Age:	17 or younger	3.8333
	18-20	3.3248
	21-29	3.3212
	30-39	3.3416
	40-49	3.7604
	50-59	3.8645
	60 or older	3.6818
Class Rank:	Freshman	3.4368
	Sophomore	3.4168
	Junior	3.3170
	Senior	3.2989
	Graduate Student	3.3998
	Doctoral Student	3.5706
Church Activity Hours:	Less than 1	3.3245
	1-3	3.3845
	4-7	3.3480
	8-12	3.5000
	13-20	3.5000
	More than 20	3.4942
Social Media Hours:	Less than 1	3.1022
	1-3	3.3507
	4-7	3.4014
	8-12	3.3878
	13-20	3.3753
	More than 20	3.5570
Prayed?	Yes	3.4829
	No	3.2266
Shared Faith?	Yes	3.4248
	No	3.1773
Total		**3.3831**

Table 59
Kindness

Demographic Categories	Variable	M
Gender	Male	4.0288
	Female	4.2081
Class Delivery:	On Campus	4.1137
	Online/Distance Learning	4.2149
Age:	17 or younger	4.2083
	18-20	4.1142
	21-29	4.1015
	30-39	4.0958
	40-49	4.3049
	50-59	4.2956
	60 or older	4.0667
Class Rank:	Freshman	4.1318
	Sophomore	4.1062
	Junior	4.0670
	Senior	4.1348
	Graduate Student	4.2242
	Doctoral Student	4.1702
Church Activity Hours:	Less than 1	3.9578
	1-3	4.1254
	4-7	4.1574
	8-12	4.2461
	13-20	4.2391
	More than 20	4.2299
Social Media Hours:	Less than 1	3.7500
	1-3	4.0382
	4-7	4.1424
	8-12	4.2064
	13-20	4.1675
	More than 20	4.2642
Prayed?	Yes	4.2160
	No	3.9864
Shared Faith?	Yes	4.1862
	No	3.8366
Total		**4.1265**

Table 60
Withhold Judgment

Demographic Categories	Variable	M
Gender	Male	2.6520
	Female	2.5083
Class Delivery:	On Campus	2.5509
	Online/Distance Learning	2.7305
Age:	17 or younger	2.4167
	18-20	2.4594
	21-29	2.4709
	30-39	2.6533
	40-49	3.1907
	50-59	3.1795
	60 or older	3.4419
Class Rank:	Freshman	2.6275
	Sophomore	2.5421
	Junior	2.4619
	Senior	2.4407
	Graduate Student	2.6719
	Doctoral Student	2.8889
Church Activity Hours:	Less than 1	2.5484
	1-3	2.5405
	4-7	2.5506
	8-12	2.7342
	13-20	2.7500
	More than 20	2.6766
Social Media Hours:	Less than 1	2.4728
	1-3	2.6112
	4-7	2.5413
	8-12	2.4938
	13-20	2.5462
	More than 20	2.9116
Prayed?	Yes	2.6125
	No	2.5112
Shared Faith?	Yes	2.5920
	No	2.4843
Total		**2.5736**

Table 61
Grumble

Demographic Categories	Variable	M
Gender	Male	2.7335
	Female	2.6051
Class Delivery:	On Campus	2.6298
	Online/Distance Learning	2.8993
Age:	17 or younger	2.8261
	18-20	2.5701
	21-29	2.5530
	30-39	2.8180
	40-49	3.1698
	50-59	3.2109
	60 or older	3.2821
Class Rank:	Freshman	2.7058
	Sophomore	2.6786
	Junior	2.5795
	Senior	2.5162
	Graduate Student	2.7492
	Doctoral Student	2.8718
Church Activity Hours:	Less than 1	2.6176
	1-3	2.6121
	4-7	2.6687
	8-12	2.8360
	13-20	2.9022
	More than 20	2.7607
Social Media Hours:	Less than 1	2.6250
	1-3	2.7203
	4-7	2.6903
	8-12	2.5489
	13-20	2.6037
	More than 20	2.8068
Prayed?	Yes	2.6628
	No	2.6637
Shared Faith?	Yes	2.6753
	No	2.6043
Total		**2.6633**

Table 62
Hospitable

Demographic Categories	Variable	M
Gender	Male	3.7681
	Female	3.8475
Class Delivery:	On Campus	3.7993
	Online/Distance Learning	3.8964
Age:	17 or younger	4.1250
	18-20	3.7860
	21-29	3.7616
	30-39	3.8070
	40-49	4.0364
	50-59	4.1019
	60 or older	3.9318
Class Rank:	Freshman	3.8597
	Sophomore	3.8328
	Junior	3.7706
	Senior	3.7353
	Graduate Student	3.8273
	Doctoral Student	3.9329
Church Activity Hours:	Less than 1	3.7336
	1-3	3.7745
	4-7	3.8337
	8-12	3.9522
	13-20	3.8140
	More than 20	3.9825
Social Media Hours:	Less than 1	3.5027
	1-3	3.7250
	4-7	3.8327
	8-12	3.8239
	13-20	3.9370
	More than 20	3.9452
Prayed?	Yes	3.8938
	No	3.6853
Shared Faith?	Yes	3.8743
	No	3.5058
Total		**3.8115**

Table 63
Confess sins

Demographic Categories	Variable	M
Gender	Male	3.2555
	Female	3.3011
Class Delivery:	On Campus	3.2872
	Online/Distance Learning	3.2309
Age:	17 or younger	3.8696
	18-20	3.3250
	21-29	3.2629
	30-39	3.2061
	40-49	3.2905
	50-59	3.2993
	60 or older	2.9000
Class Rank:	Freshman	3.4004
	Sophomore	3.3883
	Junior	3.2622
	Senior	3.2648
	Graduate Student	3.2061
	Doctoral Student	3.0438
Church Activity Hours:	Less than 1	3.2118
	1-3	3.3001
	4-7	3.2805
	8-12	3.3625
	13-20	3.3077
	More than 20	3.1728
Social Media Hours:	Less than 1	3.0924
	1-3	3.1989
	4-7	3.3031
	8-12	3.3333
	13-20	3.3351
	More than 20	3.3101
Prayed?	Yes	3.3808
	No	3.1226
Shared Faith?	Yes	3.3239
	No	3.0635
Total		**3.2802**

Table 64
Carry burdens

Demographic Categories	Variable	M
Gender	Male	3.9002
	Female	3.9799
Class Delivery:	On Campus	3.9096
	Online/Distance Learning	4.1812
Age:	17 or younger	4.0833
	18-20	3.8443
	21-29	3.9098
	30-39	4.0050
	40-49	4.3073
	50-59	4.3077
	60 or older	4.0435
Class Rank:	Freshman	3.9058
	Sophomore	3.8978
	Junior	3.8317
	Senior	3.8831
	Graduate Student	4.0602
	Doctoral Student	4.2242
Church Activity Hours:	Less than 1	3.6341
	1-3	3.9365
	4-7	4.0070
	8-12	4.1281
	13-20	4.0556
	More than 20	4.2544
Social Media Hours:	Less than 1	3.6828
	1-3	3.9365
	4-7	3.9858
	8-12	3.9812
	13-20	3.9373
	More than 20	3.8810
Prayed?	Yes	4.0593
	No	3.7672
Shared Faith?	Yes	3.9959
	No	3.6898
Total		**3.9438**

Table 65
Warn

Demographic Categories	Variable	M
Gender	Male	3.6100
	Female	3.5406
Class Delivery:	On Campus	3.5512
	Online/Distance Learning	3.7191
Age:	17 or younger	3.9583
	18-20	3.5775
	21-29	3.5347
	30-39	3.5840
	40-49	3.6667
	50-59	3.7647
	60 or older	3.2791
Class Rank:	Freshman	3.7289
	Sophomore	3.6197
	Junior	3.4565
	Senior	3.4369
	Graduate Student	3.6021
	Doctoral Student	3.6606
Church Activity Hours:	Less than 1	3.4901
	1-3	3.5360
	4-7	3.5932
	8-12	3.6426
	13-20	3.6304
	More than 20	3.8497
Social Media Hours:	Less than 1	3.3911
	1-3	3.5340
	4-7	3.5874
	8-12	3.5730
	13-20	3.6111
	More than 20	3.6826
Prayed?	Yes	3.6359
	No	3.4722
Shared Faith?	Yes	3.6340
	No	3.2694
Total		**3.5724**

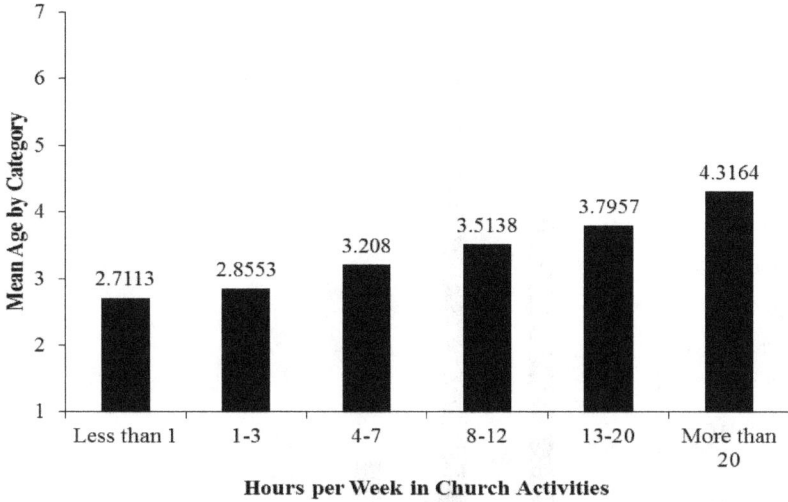

Figure 1. Mean ages for respondents based on the number of hours they spent each week in church activities.

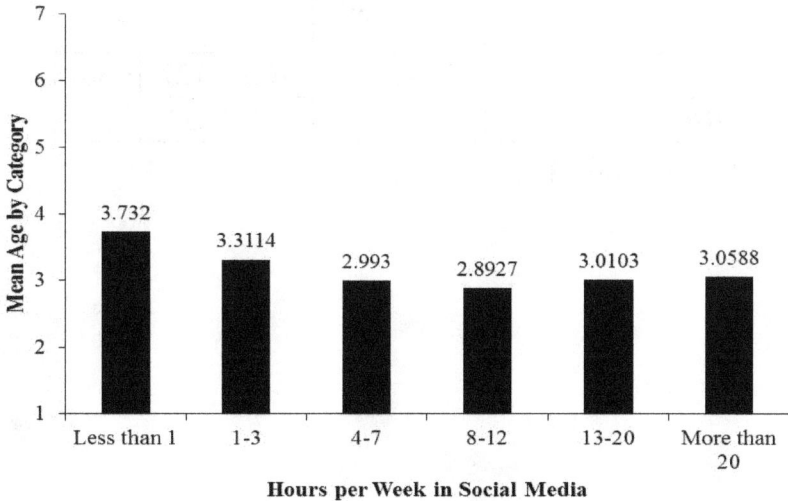

Figure 2. Mean ages for respondents based on the number of hours they spent each week in social media activities.

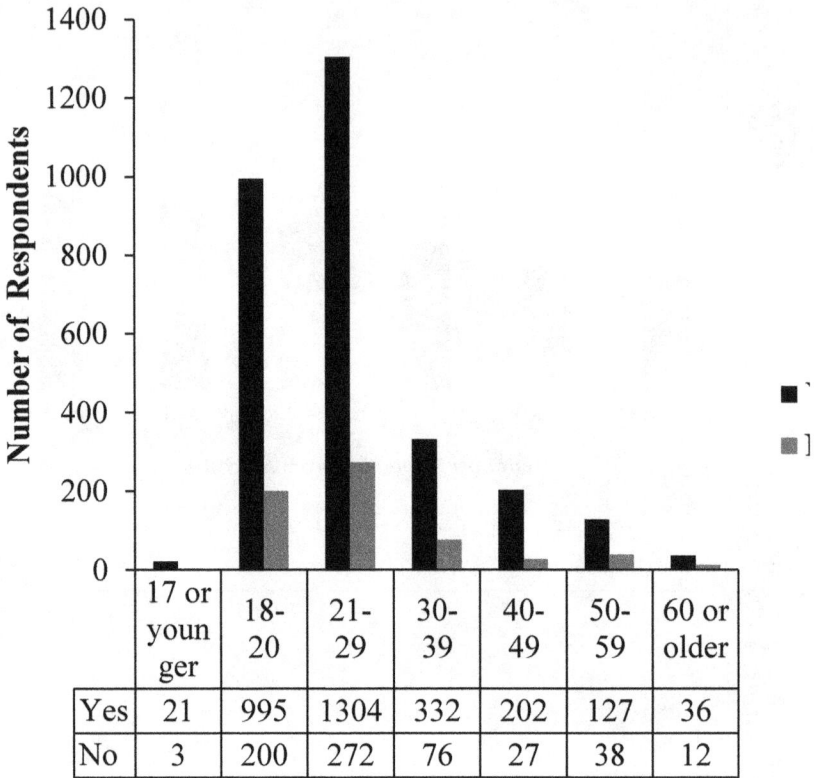

	17 or younger	18-20	21-29	30-39	40-49	50-59	60 or older
Yes	21	995	1304	332	202	127	36
No	3	200	272	76	27	38	12

Figure 3. Have you shared your faith through social media?

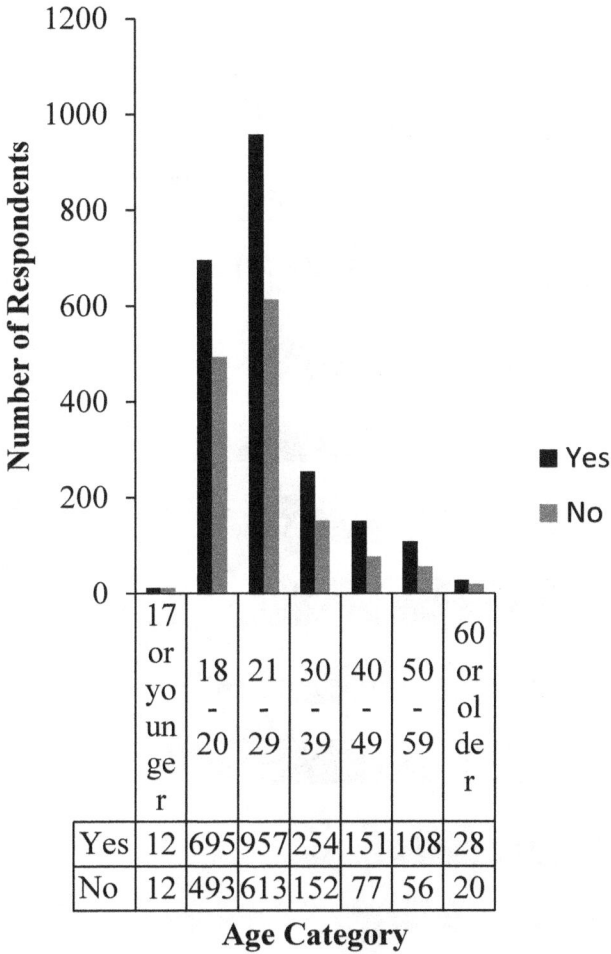

	17 or younger	18 - 20	21 - 29	30 - 39	40 - 49	50 - 59	60 or older
Yes	12	695	957	254	151	108	28
No	12	493	613	152	77	56	20

Age Category

Figure 4. Have you prayed with someone using social media?

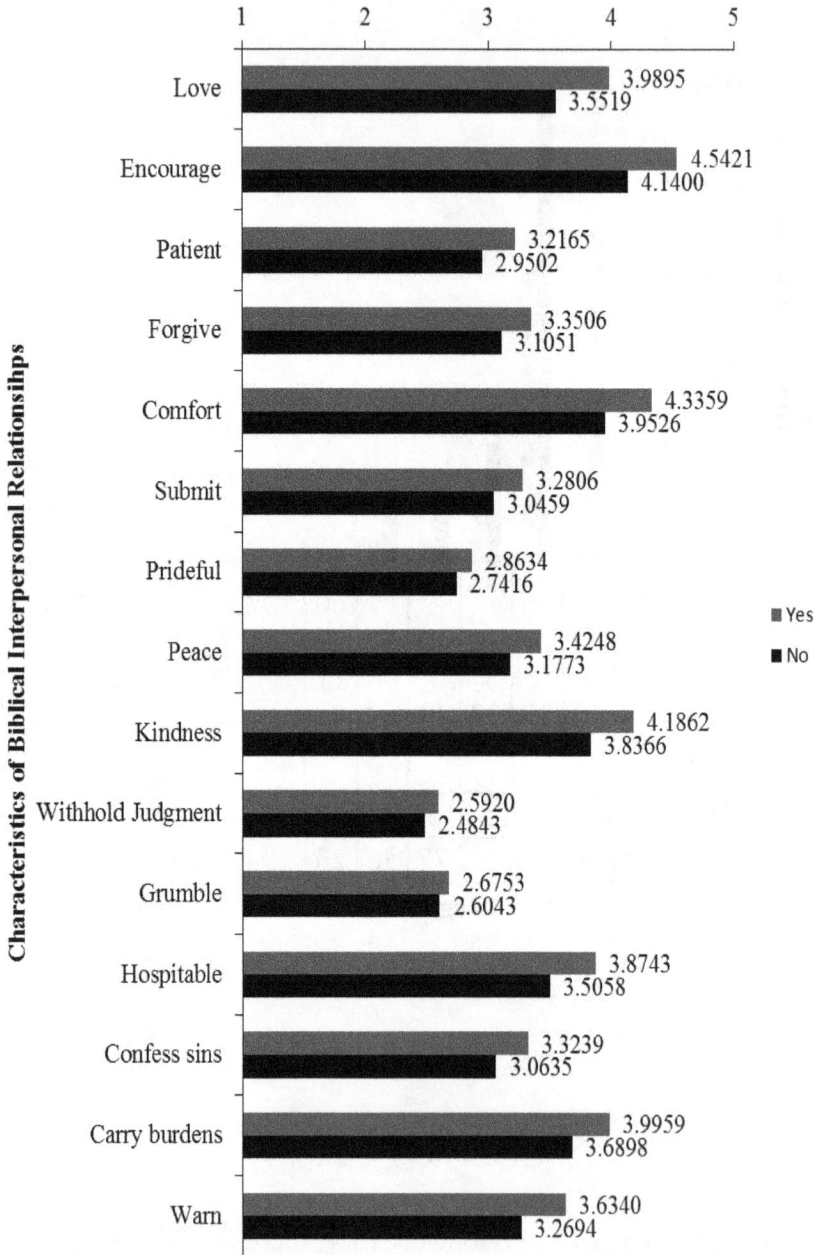

Figure 5. Have you shared your faith through social media?

REFERENCES

Akin, D. L. (2009, June 6). *Marks of A Healthy Community of Faith*. Retrieved June 1, 2011, from Daniel Akin: President of Southeastern Baptist Theological Seminary: http://www.danielakin.com/?p=1258

American Psychiatric Association. (2000). *Diagnostic and Statistical Manual of Mental Disorders* (4 ed.). Washington, DC: American Psychiatric Publishers.

Anderson, B., & Tracey, K. (2001). Digital living: the impact (or otherwise) of the internet on everyday life. *American Behavioral Scientist, 45*(3), 456-475.

Auday, B. C., & Coleman, S. W. (2009). Pulling off the mask: The impact of social networking activities on evangelical Christian college students. 1-9.

Bargh, J. A., & McKenna, K. Y. (2004). The internet and social life. *The Annual Review of Psychology, 55*, 573-590.

Bargh, J. A., McKenna, K. Y., & Fitzsimons, G. M. (2002). Can you see the real me? activation and expression of the "true self" on the internet. *The Society for the Psychological Study of Social Issues, 58*(1), 33-48.

Berkman, L. F., & Glass, T. A. (2000). Social intergration, social networks, social support and health. In L. F. Berkman, & I. Kawachi (Eds.), *Social epidemiology* (pp. 137-74). New York: Oxford Press.

Bobkowski, P. S., & Kalyanaraman, S. (2010). Effects of online Christian self--disclosure on impression formation. *Journal for the Scientific Study of Religion, 49*(3), 456-476.

Bock, D. (2007). *Acts.* (R. W. Yarbrough, & R. H. Stein, Eds.) Grand Rapids: Baker.

Boice, J. M. (1976). Galatians. In F. E. Gaebelein (Ed.), *The Expositor's Bible Commentary* (Vol. 10, pp. 407-508). Grand Rapids: Zondervan.

Bolsinger, T. E. (2004). *It Takes a Church to Raise a Christian: How the Community of God Transforms Lives.* Grand Rapids: Brazos.

Bonhoeffer, D. (1954). Community. In *Life Together* (J. W. Doberstein, Trans., pp. 17-39). New York: Harper & Row.

Brehm, S. S., Miller, R. S., Perlman, D., & Campbell, S. M. (2002). The Building Blocks of Relationships. In P. G. Zimbardo (Ed.), *Intimate Relationships* (3 ed., pp. xv-34). New York: McGraw-Hill Higher Education.

Brock, B. (2010). *Christian Ethics in a Technological Age.* Grand Rapids: Wm. B. Eerdmans Publishing.

Brown, J. D., & Bobkowski, P. S. (2011). Older and news media: patterns of use and effects on adolescents' health and well-being. *Journal of Research on Adolescence, 21*(1), 95-113.

Bruce, F. F. (1982). *1 & 2 Thessalonians.* (B. M. Metzger, R. P. Martin, & L. A. Losie, Eds.) Nashville: Thomas Nelson.

Calvin, J. (1984). *James.* (J. Owen, Trans.) Grand Rapids: Baker.

Calvin, J. (1984). The Espistle of James. In J. Owen (Ed.), *Calvin's Commentaries* (J. Owen, Trans., Vol. 22, pp. 276-362). Baker: Grand Rapids.

Carr, N. (2010). *The Shallows: What the Internet is doing to Our Brains.* New York: W.W. Norton & Company.

Carson, D. (2005, March). *On Being Prepared for Suffering and Evil pt. 1.* Denver Seminary Chapel, Denver, CO.

Challies, T. (2011). *The Next Story: Life and Faith After the Digital Explosion.* Grand Rapids: Zondervan.

Clough, D. (2000). The message of the medium: the challenge of the internet to the church and other communities. *Studies in Christian Ethics, 13*(2), 91-100.

Correa, T., Hinsley, A. W., & Zuniga, H. G. (2010). Who interacts on the Web?: the intersection of users' personality and social media use. *Computers in HUman Behavior, 26,* 247-253.

Cosgrove, F. M. (1978). The Church and Christian Community. In *Essentials of New Life: Biblical Truths a new Christian Needs to Know* (pp. 97-116). Colorado Springs: NavPress.

Cummings, J. N., Butler, B., & Kraut, R. (2000). The quality of online social relationships. *Communications of the ACM, 45*(7), 103-108.

Davids, P. H. (1989). *James* (Vol. 15). (W. W. Gasque, Ed.) Peabody: Hendrickson.

Dever, M. (2004). A Biblical Understanding of Church Membership. In *9 Marks of a Healthy Church* (2 ed., pp. 147-65). Wheaton: Crossway.

Dever, M. (2009). Autonomy. In *Twelve Challenges Churches Face* (pp. 111-25). Wheaton: Crossway.

Driscoll, M., & Breshears, G. (2010). Church: God Sends. In *Doctrine: What Christians Should Believe* (pp. 305-36). Wheaton: Crossway.

Dwyer, C., Hiltz, S. R., & Passerini, K. (2007). Trust privacy concern within social networking sites: a comparison of facebook and myspace. (pp. 1-11). Keystone, CO: Thirteenth Americas Conference on Information Systems .

Dyer, J. (2011). *From the Garden to the City.* Grand Rapids: Kregel.

Ellison, N. B., Steinfield, C., & Lampe, C. (2007). The benefits of facebook "friends:" social capital and college students' use of online social network sites. *The Journal of Computer-Mediated Communication, 12*, 1143-1168.

Estes, D. (2009). *SimChurch: Being the Church in the Virtual World.* Grand Rapids: Zondervan.

Foulkes, F. (1989). *Ephesians* (Vol. 10). (L. Morris, Ed.) Downers Grove: InterVarsity.

Gilbert, G. (2010). Keeping the Cross at the Center. In *What is the Gospel* (pp. 101-13). Wheaton: Crossway.

Green, M. (1992). Fellowship. In *Evangelism Throught the Local Church: A Comprehensive Guide to All Aspects of Evangelism* (pp. 298-99). Nashville: Oliver-Nelson.

Grenz, S. J. (1996). In *Created for Community* (pp. 9-27, 252-298). Grand Rapids: Baker.

Grudem, W. (1988). *1 Peter* (Vol. 17). (L. Morris, Ed.) Downers Grove: InterVarsity Press.

Grudem, W. (1994). Fellowship. In *Systematic Theology: An Introduction to Biblical Doctrine* (pp. 958-59). Grand Rapids: Zondervan.

Grudem, W. (1994). Personal Fellowship with Christ. In *Systematic Theology: An Introduction to Biblical Doctrine* (pp. 846-47). Grand Rapids: Zondervan.

Hammett, J. S. (2007). Human Nature. In D. L. Akin (Ed.), *A Theology for the Church* (pp. 340-408). Nashville: B&H Publishing.

Hampton, K., & Wellman, B. (2003). Neighboring in netville: how the internet supports community and social capital in a wired suburb. *City & Community, 2*(4), 277-311.

Harris, J. (2004). In *Stop Dating the Church: Fall in Love with the Family of God* (pp. 63-81). Colorado Springs: Multnomah.

Harrison, E. F. (1976). Romans. In F. E. Gæbelien (Ed.), *Expositor's Bible Commentary* (1 ed., Vol. 10). Grand Rapids: Zondervan.

Haythornthwaite, C. (2001). Introduction: the internet in everyday life. *American Behavioral Scientist, 45*(3), 363-382.

Heinemann, M. H. (2007). Teacher-student integration and learning in online theological education. Part four: findings and conclusions. *Christian Higher Education, 6*, 185-206.

Hemphill, K. (2008). Characteristic 5 -- Nurturing Biblical Fellowship. In *Eternal Impact* (pp. 108-115). Nashville: B&H Publishers.

Hendricks, G. A. (1986). *To Higher Ground: A Biography of High Shoal Baptist Church*. Rutherfordton: Liberty Press.

Hendriksen, W. (1967). *Exposition of Ephesians*. Grand Rapids: Baker.

Hendriksen, W. (1968). *Exosition of Galatians*. Grand Rapids: Baker Books.

Holmes, M. W. (1998). *1 & 2 Thessalonians*. (T. Muck, Ed.) Grand Rapids: Zondervan.

Hunter, G. G. (2000). In *The Celtic Way of Evangelism: How Christianity Can Reach the West...Again* (pp. 9-35). Nashville: Abingdon.

Jarvis, L. A. (1999). *Galatians* (Vol. 9). (W. W. Gasque, Ed.) Peabody: Hendrickson.

Jobes, K. H. (2005). *1 Peter*. (R. W. Yarbrough, & R. H. Stein, Eds.) Grand Rapids: Baker Academic.

Kelly, D. F., Rollinson, P. B., & Marsh, F. T. (1986). *The Westminster Shorter Catechism in Modern English*. Phillipsburg: Presbyterian and Reformed Pub. Co.

Kelly, J. N. (1987). *A Commentary on the Epistles of Peter and Jude*. Grand Rapids: Baker.

Kostenberger, A. J. (2004). *John.* Grand Rapids: Baker Academic.

Kraut, R., Patterson, M. , Lundmark, V., Kiesler, S., Mukopadhyay, T., & Scherlis, W. (1998). Internet paradox: a social technology that reduces social invlovement and psychological well-being? *American Psychologist, 53*(9), 1017-1031.

Ladd, G. E. (1974). In *A Theology of the New Testament* (pp. 348-54). Grand Rapids: Eerdmans.

Helgeland, B. (Director). (2002). *A Knight's Tale* [Motion Picture].

Leeman, J. (2010). The Affirmation and Witness of Love. In *The Church and the Surprising Offense of God's Love: Reintroducing the Doctrines of Church Membership and Discipline* (pp. 273-323). Wheaton: Crossway.

Lincoln, A. T. (1990). *Ephesians* (Vol. 42). (B. M. Metzger, R. M. Martin, & L. A. Losie, Eds.) Waco: Word.

Long, J. (2004). Emerging Hope. In *Emerging Hope: A Strategy for Reaching Postmodern Generations* (pp. 89-102). Downers Grove: InterVarsity Press.

Malphurs, A. (2007). The Changing Church: Developing a Theology of Change. In *A New Kind of Church* (pp. 75-94). Grand Rapids: Baker.

Malta, S. (2007). Love actually! older aults and their romantic internet relationships. *Australian Journal of Emerging Technologies and Society, 5*(2), 84-103.

McCullar, S. (2002). The Path of Membership in the Early Church. *Faith & Mission*, 19-25.

McKenna, K. Y., & Green, A. S. (2002). Virtual group dynamics. *Educational Publishing Foundation, 6*(1), 116-127.

McKenna, K. Y., Green, A. S., & Gleason, M. E. (2002). Relationship formation on the internet: what's the big attraction? *The Society for the Psychological Study of Social Issues, 58*(1), 9-31.

McRay, J. (2001). Fellowship. In W. A. Elwell (Ed.), *Evangelical Dictionary of Theology* (2 ed., p. 445). Grand Rapids: Baker.

Mesch, G. (2005). A study of adolescents' online and offline social relationships. *Oxford Internet Institute, 8*, 1-24.

Mesch, G. S. (2001). Social relationships and internet use among adolescents in Israel. *Social Science Quarterly, 82*(2), 329-339.

Migliore, D. L. (2004). The New Community. In *Faith Seeking Understanding: An Introduction to Christian Theology* (2 ed., pp. 248-73). Grand Rapids: Eerdmans.

Mohler, R. A. (2009). In *The Disapperance of God: Dangerous Beliefs in the New Spiritual Openness* (pp. 3-12). Colorado Springs: Multnomah.

Moore, R. (2004). Toward a Kingdom Ecclesiology. In *The Kingdom of Christ: The New Evangelical Perspective* (pp. 131-73). Wheaton: Crossway.

Moriarty, G. (2005). 5loaves.net - a Christain social network: definitions, development, and survey results. *Journal of Religion and Popular Culture, 11*(Fall), 1-17. Retrieved 10 11, 2012, from http://www.usask.ca/relst/jrpc/art11-5loaves-print.html

Morris, J. M., Beck, R., & Smith, A. B. (2004). Examining student/institution fit at a Christian university: the role of spiritual integration. *Journal of Education & Christian Belief, 8*(2), 87-100.

Morris, L. (1988). *The Epistle to the Romans*. Grand Rapids: Eerdmans.

Nie, N. H., Hillygus, D. S., & Erbring, L. (2002). Internet use, interpersonal relations, and sociability. *IT & Society, 1*(1), 1-20.

Norman, R. S. (2005). Congregational Polity. In *The Baptist Way* (pp. 84-110). Nashville: B&H Publishers.

Patzia, A. G. (1990). Colossians. In W. W. Gasque (Ed.), *Ephesians, Colossians, Philemon* (Vol. 10). Peabody: Hendrickson.

Philadelphia Baptist Confession of Faith. (2007). Asheville: Revival Literature.

Rice, J. (2009). *The Church of Facebook.* Colorado Springs: David C. Cook.

Sarriera, J. C., Abs, D., Casas, F., & Bedin, L. M. (2012). Relations between media, perceived social support and personal well-being in adolescence. *Social Indicators Research, 106*, 545-561.

Schaeffer, F. (1998). *The God Who is There.* Downers Grove: InterVarsity Press.

Schaeffer, F. (2006). In *The Mark of the Christian* (2 ed., pp. 7-59). Downers Grove: InterVarsity Press.

Segler, F. M., & Bradley, R. (2006). Community and Worship. In *Christian Worship: Its Theology and Practice* (pp. 81-89). Nashville: B&H Publishing.

Shklovski, I., Kiesler, S., & Kraut, R. (2006). The internet and social interaction: a meta-analysis and critique of studies, 1995-2003. In R. Kraut, M. Brynin, & S. Kiesler (Eds.), *Computers, Phones and the Internet: Domesticating Information Technology* (pp. 251-264). New York: Oxford University Press.

Stetzer, E. (2003). In *Planting Churches in a Postmodern Age* (pp. 136-56). Nashville: B&H Publishers.

Stetzer, E. (2007). Connecting People through Small Groups. In *Comeback Churches: How 300 Churches Turned Around and Yours Can Too* (pp. 146-61). Nashville: B&H Publishing.

Stott, J. R. (1989). *The Letters of John* (Vol. 19). (L. Morris, Ed.) Downers Grove, Il: IVP Academic.

Strom, M. (2000). Frames for New Community. In *Reframing Paul: Conversations in Grace & Community* (pp. 167-81). Downers Grove: InterVarsity Press.

Struthers, W. M. (2009). *Wired for Initmacy: How pornography hijacks the male brain.* InterVaristy Press: Downers Grove.

Tasker, R. V. (1976). *The General Epistle of James.* Grand Rapids: Wm. B. Eerdmans Publishing.

Turkle, S. (2001). *Alone Together.* New York: Basic Books.

United States Census Bureau. (2010). Reported Activity of People Using the Internet, by Selected Individual Characteristics. from https://www.census.gov/hhes/computer/publications/2010.html

Underwoord, H., & Findlay, B. (2004). Internet relationships and their impact on primary relationships. *Behaviour Change, 21*(2), 127-140.

Vaughan, C. (1890). Church Life. In *The Church of the First Days* (2 ed., pp. 41-50). New York: Macmillan and Co.

Walton, J. H. (2001). *Genesis* (Vol. 1). (T. Muck, Ed.) Grand Rapids: Zondervan.

Weizenbaum, J. (1976). *Computer Power and Human Reason: From Judgment to Calculation*. New York: W.H. Freeman.

Williams, D. J. (1992). *1 and 2 Thessalonians* (Vol. 12). (W. W. Gasque, Ed.) Peabody: Hendrickson.

Witmer, T. Z. (2010). In *The Shepherd Leader: Achieving Effective Shepherding in Your Church* (pp. 193-224). Phillipsburg: P&R Publishing.

ABOUT THE AUTHOR

Micheal S. Pardue, Sr. is President of Educational Design and Development, serves as the pastor of First Baptist Church Icard, NC and has served five other churches in the Foothills of North Carolina. Micheal holds a Master of Christian Ministry from the T. Walter Brashier Graduate School at North Greenville University and a Doctorate of Education from Southeastern Baptist Theological Seminary. He is currently pursuing a Doctorate of Ministry in Preaching from Southeastern Baptist Theological Seminary.

Dr. Pardue has had the privilege of speaking in more than thirty churches, colleges, and Baptist associations across North Carolina, South Carolina, and Virginia. He serves as President of the Pastor's Conference on of the Baptist State Convention of North Carolina. He is also an Instructor for Liberty University.

Micheal writes for both the North Carolina Biblical Recorder and for the Blue Ridge Christian News.

He and his wife, Rachel, have seven children: Elijah, Jason, Kyle, Kristen, Addelyen, Lilyanna, and Micheal, Jr. For more information about Micheal and his writing go to www.michealpardue.com or follow him on Twitter @michealpardue.

9 780692 302163